Sand in My Bra

"Twenty-eight short and snappy travel stories bursting with exuberant candor and crackling humor sure to leave readers feeling that to not have an adventure to remember is a great loss indeed."

— *Publishers Weekly*

There's No Toilet Paper…on the Road Less Traveled

"There is a point, somewhere beyond frustration but before hari-kiri, where the only sensible way to confront the vagaries of travel is with humor. So if you find yourself teetering precariously close to the edge, take an immediate dose of *There's No Toilet Paper….*"

— *Trips*

Not So Funny When It Happened

"A noted travel writer himself, Tim Cahill has collected the best humorous travel pieces in one funny-bone volume."

— *Chicago Tribune*

"These stories are humorous, indeed. In a few cases the reader may have gone through a similar agonizing experience—one that was not the least bit funny at the time, but comical to look back on."

— *Booklist*

Last Trout in Venice

"This rich and hilarious collection…is sure to inspire readers to 'just go' and create their own unforgettable experiences on the road. From sashaying through Berlin's Kit Kat Club in a one-piece latex suit to working as a bellhop in the world's only underwater hotel, Doug Lansky is willing to try anything."

— Eric Kettunen, Lonely Planet Publications

The Fire Never Dies

"…offering an audacious recounting of…macho-gastro-comical adventures tinged with equal parts of pathos, earthy humor and just a pinch of malarkey may be just the right recipe to kick start jaded taste buds to new heights."

— *Frequent Flyer Online*

TRAVELERS' TALES

HYENAS
Laughed at Me
and Now I Know Why

The Best of Travel Humor
and Misadventure

HYENAS
Laughed at Me
and Now I Know Why

The Best of Travel Humor
and Misadventure

Edited by

SEAN O'REILLY, LARRY HABEGGER,
AND JAMES O'REILLY

TRAVELERS' TALES

SAN FRANCISCO

Art Direction: Michele Wetherbee
Interior design: Kathryn Heflin and Susan Bailey
Cover photograph: © *Mitsuaki Iwago/Minden Pictures. Spotted Hyena (Crocuta crocuta)*
Page layout: Patty Holden using the fonts Bembo, Journal, and Boulevard

Distributed by: Publishers Group West, 1700 Fourth Street, Berkeley, California 94710.

Library of Congress Cataloguing-in-Publication Data

Hyenas laughed at me, and now I know why : the best of travel humor and misadventure / edited by Sean O'Reilly, Larry Habegger, and James O'Reilly— 1st ed.
    p. cm.
At head of title: Travelers' Tales.
  ISBN 1-885211-97-X (pbk.)
  1. Travel—Anecdotes. 2. Travelers—Anecdotes. I. Title: Travelers' Tales, hyenas laughed at me, and now I know why. II. O'Reilly, Sean. III. Habegger, Larry. IV. O'Reilly, James, 1953–
G151.H94 2003
910.4—dc22

                2003019955

First Edition
Printed in the United States
10 9 8 7 6 5 4 3 2 1

I looked out the tent at the hyena: fierce, hungry, and determined—
but probably dumb enough to outwit. I looked down at Saskia in her
sleeping bag: intelligent, unpredictable, and female—with needs and
desires no safari guide could explain. She seemed innocent enough:
tall, blond, smiling, playful. But compared to what she wants, the
hyena is Lassie. What she wants makes men run down the street with
their arms flailing, it brings them to their knees begging for mercy:
she wants to talk. She wants me to open up to her, to let her into
my feelings, to spill my secrets, and talk about our relationship.
Africa was desperate, violent, and dangerous. I was only
desperate. The hyena laughed, and I wondered why.

—Bradley Charbonneau, Our Country

Table of Contents

Hyenas Laughed at Me and Now I Know Why
An Introduction
TIM CAHILL

Introducing this book of humorous travel essays by many fine authors offers me the opportunity to engage in a lot of pious plagiarism. I could very easily climb up on the shoulders of these other writers and give away their best lines, their most outrageous situations: I could, in short, delineate the very circumstances that will often make you laugh out loud while reading the book. In this manner—call it unscrupulous theft—I could make myself appear to be quite an amusing fellow.

There are two reasons why I will not do this.

1. It is morally reprehensible.
2. The editors won't let me.

In any case, most of these articles do not lend themselves to easy pilfering. This is to say, there are not a lot of one liners here. (Doug Lansky is the reliable exception.) In most of the essays, situations develop, circumstances deepen, plots thicken. In Patrick Fitzhugh's "The Snake Charmer of Guanacaste" a giant drunken Russian weight lifter encounters one of the world's deadliest snakes. Doesn't sound funny on the face of it? I laughed out loud on a crowded airplane.

Even forthright adventures such as riding the rails like the hobos of old present odd obstacles to certain writers, at least

to Jennifer L. Leo, who masquerades as a man in the
interests of personal safety. Read all about it in "Boxcar Steve."

Female adventurers abound in this collection. Western
readers of any gender will learn that sometimes just buying
a bra can be an occasion of exquisite cross-cultural embarrassment as it was for Jacqueline C. Yau, as described in "King
Kong in Shanghai."

I will say, in perfect introductory candor, that not all the
stories are outright knee slappers. Every single one, however,
is fascinating in and of itself. I especially liked Richard
Sterling's "Saigon Games," but it didn't make me laugh. (I
gave it to a friend whose taste I admire and she giggled
through the whole thing. There's no accounting for taste.)

Similarly, I would also advise the reader not to give up on
a tale. Sometimes it is necessary to comprehend various important taboos and rituals to understand how the writer
eventually made a complete ass of himself or herself.

And yes, they almost always make asses of themselves. I
suspect the writers, in many cases, wrote these stories as an
act of therapy, in the full understanding that only time and
the pen can elevate humiliation to humor. I like to think of
this process as the revenge of the mortified.

Indeed, I was reading one tale in which Bennett Stevens,
a man apparently bereft of any cultural sensitivity whatsoever, resolves to photograph "the single largest gathering of
humanity the planet has ever known" and ends up suffering
an occasion of mind-numbing disgrace. I'd tell you about it
here, but the editors won't let me.

There is at least one legendary piece in the book, and that
is "A Bard in the Bush." This is the introduction to a memoir by the well-known war correspondent, Thomas Goltz.
The book is unpublished for reasons that remain opaque to

me. In it, Goltz casts back twenty years to relate tales from his first trip through Africa, which he financed, on the spot, by performing scenes from Shakespearean plays on the street. Turns out you can get arrested for that—"was my Hamlet that bad?"—because, in the end, Shakespeare's tales of kingly usurpation and assassinations still run uncomfortably close to the truth even in Africa, or perhaps especially in Africa.

Indeed, the best of these stories open up our worlds and our minds. In "Cowboys and Indians, Thai Style," Rolf Potts *purposely* goes to a Western-themed "ranch" in Thailand where he is subjected to a dramatic entertainment featuring "drunk man cowboy and his gang." Lots of people get beaten up, especially those dressed as Indians, and it would be easy, Potts decides, to see all this as a "distinctly negative symptom of cultural globalization." Well, of course it is, but there's more to it and Potts finds himself wondering if "Californians who seek solace in Nepali ashrams" are truly experiencing superior cross-cultural authenticity.

This is funny stuff, all of it, but only because it is true, and that is the point of each and every story here.

Tim Cahill is the author of many books, mostly travel-related, including Hold the Enlightenment, Jaguars Ripped My Flesh, Pecked to Death by Ducks, Pass the Butterworms, *and* Dolphins, *as well as the editor of* Not So Funny When it Happened: The Best of Travel Humor and Misadventure. *Cahill is also the co-author of the Academy Award-nominated IMAX film,* The Living Sea, *as well as the films* Everest *and* Dolphins. *He lives in Montana, and shares his life with Linnea Larson, two dogs, and two cats.*

ELLIOTT HESTER

⁎

When Fists Flew on the San Juan Special

Round two goes to the hat man.

BACK WHEN DC-10S ROAMED THE AIR SPACE BETWEEN NEW York and Puerto Rico, when I was new with the airline, when the world lay before me like a virgin wearing nothing but a wicked grin, I worked, on occasion, the most dreaded of all flights: the infamous San Juan Special. The S.J.S. had the dubious distinction of departing from JFK shortly before midnight, seven days a week, 365 days a year. It was always filled to capacity with 295 cut-rate passengers who didn't give a damn about the 3:30 A.M. arrival time. What mattered was the ninety-nine dollar one-way airfare.

Only the hardiest flight attendants remained mentally and physically unscathed after working a typical three-and-a half-hour flight. The Saturday night departure (a.k.a. the Saturday Night Special) was particularly rough. It seemed there was always a fight, always a problem, always an incident to add to the pages of airline folklore.

On one particularly comical Saturday Night Special, I watched a new flight attendant suffer a nervous breakdown while she collected tickets at the boarding gate. A hoard of overanxious New Yorkers—the likes of whom the poor, naïve Texas girl had never seen—descended upon her, trying to board the airplane all at once. From my faraway position at the aircraft end of the jet bridge, I could barely make out her frantic shouts: "Please…please, back up," she cried. "Y'all listen to me…nooooooo!"

Forgoing my assigned position at the aircraft entry door, I stepped into the jet bridge, looked down the corridor and saw one of the strangest sights of my airline career. The flight attendant was sprinting toward me—arms flailing, knees pumping, big hair splashing around her head like a waterfall gone berserk. A herd of heckling passengers crossed the jet bridge in pursuit.

"They won't listen to me, they won't listen to me," she cried.

"*They won't listen to me, they won't listen to me*," mocked a voice from the approaching crowd.

Riotous laughter erupted inside the jet bridge, but from the flight attendant's perspective, the eruption might just as well have come from a volcano. Crazy with panic, she shifted into overdrive. I had no idea a country gal could run so fast wearing three pounds of makeup and two-and-a-half-inch heels. She seemed to be more than ten feet away when she launched herself, flinging her arms and legs around me as if I were a soldier returning from war and she was the expectant fiancée. Sobbing uncontrollably, twin rivers of snot running from her flaring nostrils, she trembled like scrub brush in a cold Siberian breeze.

With the hysterical flight attendant still glued to me, and a smile struggling to blossom on my pseudoserious face, I announced to the passengers that boarding would commence in a moment. They waited impatiently—smirking, rolling their eyes, jostling for position with an elbow or a knee—while a co-worker escorted the traumatized flight attendant to a lavatory where she could collect herself. But she never did. The very next day she submitted her resignation and returned home to Texas, where only the cattle stampede.

Such was life on the San Juan Special. The passengers ate you up and spat you out; only the strong survived.

During the beverage service, it was not unusual for a female passenger to demand a can of Coca-Cola. Not for herself, mind you. The high-octane soft drink was to be fed to her infant child. S.J.S. flight attendants have been known to shake their head and sigh while pouring oceans of Classic Coke into baby bottles. I've done so many times myself. To add insult to a very possible long-term injury, the same retro-mommy might request five or six packs of sugar which would be torn open, poured into the baby bottle filled with Coke, and then, like a tit plump with sugar and caffeine and carefully balanced phosphoric acid, the bottle would be jammed into the screaming infant's mouth.

At any time during the flight you might witness a card game with serious money involved. Gold chains flashed on a regular basis. Boom boxes, while not uncommon, had the uncommon habit of blasting music loud enough for everyone to hear. Rumor had it that on one exceptionally rambunctious flight, a group of hookers worked the coach-class lavatories. Passengers who wished to use the lavs for conventional purposes simply had to wait.

Patience never fared well on the San Juan Special, however. Whenever the lavs were occupied, even when alleged hookers weren't on board, passengers sometime found creative ways to purge their swollen bladders. Once, I saw a man standing absently, a few feet away from the lavatory. Upon closer inspection, I realized he was peeing into a free-standing garbage bag. As if squirted from a figurine in some debauched European fountain, the golden arc of fluid glistened in dim light that, for one fleeting moment, made the lurid scene appear respectable.

Considering the distance between man and bag, the passenger was blessed with remarkable aim and trajectory. Had we been young boys engaged in a peeing contest, I might have been impressed. But we were grown men on a goddamn airplane. I walked up beside him, threw up my hands in exasperation and said, "What the hell are you doing?" He tossed a sidelong glance, nodded his head and smiled the blissful smile of a man who had finally found relief.

On one of my very first Saturday Night Specials, airport security was summoned to the departure gate to break up an airplane brawl. The fight was initiated during the boarding process, by two men who, as children, probably suckled hundreds of Coke-filled baby bottles and pissed liquid sugar well into their thirties.

Here's how the action unfolded.

I watched a nervous-looking gentleman as he placed his new Panama hat in the overhead bin. Noting the tremendous care he bestowed upon the hat—the meticulous placement of it, the way he moved it a few inches to the left, turned it slightly, then moved it a few inches to the right—I couldn't help but smile. This was a man who loved his hat, a man whose hat was as precious as a newborn child. Clearly, this hat was not to be touched by the unsavory hands of strangers. Though the overhead bin was otherwise empty, the man closed it gently, leaving his prize to rest in uncluttered peace.

I was standing at the rear of the airplane, about twenty-five feet away from the hat man, when a heavy-set gentleman plopped into the last row of seats. His eyes were red. He stank of liquor. He was sweating and panting and seemed on the verge of collapse. Still, he looked up at me and smiled. "Psssssst, pssssst…" he said. "*Yo necsesito un vaso con hielo* [I need a glass with ice]." He opened his jacket, pointing somewhat stealth-ily to a fifth of rum tucked in his breast pocket. "*Yo necesito un vaso con hielo*," he repeated. "Ahhh, ha, ha, ha, ha, ha…"

This was the kind of passenger we occasionally greeted on the Saturday Night Special—a tipsy traveler impressed by his own resourcefulness.

As the final passengers squeezed into the crowded cabin, I noticed a man dragging a heavy carry-on bag along the right-hand aisle of the aircraft. He hurled repeated insults at his wife, who, though she was half the size of her husband, was dragging a carry-on that seemed twice as heavy as his. His wife snapped back at him, delivering a Spanish-speaking retort that sent ripples of laughter through the crowd of nearby passengers. Embarrassed by this public display of female disobedience, the husband flew into a frenzy. He yelled and cursed, berating her with a volley of conjugated verbs that drew ice-cold stares from passengers. In the midst of his tirade, the husband threw open an overhead bin. In one blind movement, he picked up his massive carry-on bag and slammed it in the overhead bin, directly on top of the pre-cious Panama hat.

The hat man sat still in his seat, frozen momentarily by the ramifications of this callous act. When the paralysis finally broke, he leapt to his feet, cursed the assailant, then reached beneath the bag to extract what was left of his hat. To his horror, the crown had been completely crushed so that now it was level to the brim. It looked like a broken Frisbee. Like a nest built by druggie sparrows.

The hat man's jaw came unhinged. He began to tremble. His eyes filled with something more complex than rage. Without taking a breath, the hat man spat a fusillade of insults in Spanish. The husband responded with a foul-mouthed blast of his own. Their shouts attracted the attention of everyone on board, including first-class passengers who were poking their heads in the aisle, trying to get a glimpse of the ruckus in the back.

I threaded my way through the crowded aisle, hoping to intervene before things got out of hand. But by the time I reached the two shouting men, the first punch had already been thrown. The hat man had been leveled by a vicious right cross.

A collective gasp seemed to suck the air out of the cavernous DC-10 cabin. Many of the 295 passengers and 10 crew members froze in their places. There was no sound. The seconds floated by like Goodyear blimps. Like a heavyweight champion refusing to be beaten by a ten-count, the hat man rose slowly from the floor. He massaged his chin for a moment, grinned sardonically, then let loose an ear-piercing battle cry:

"Hyyyyyyyyyyyyyyyyyyaaaaaaa!"

That's when all hell broke loose.

To the best of my recollection, the full-scale brawl broke out as the husband prepared to defend himself against the hat man. When hubby cocked his arm to throw another punch, his elbow inadvertently whacked the head of a seated passenger. Infuriated by this unprovoked assault, the man jumped to his feet and pushed the husband, who then fell atop a fourth man who proceeded to push the husband upon a fifth. Like the climactic scene in a Jackie Chan movie, fists were suddenly flying everywhere. Stranger battled against stranger in an aircraft skirmish fueled purely by anger and testosterone.

Not to be outdone by the guys, some of the tougher-looking female passengers joined in. I ducked beneath a misguided punch thrown by a thirty-year-old woman in a tank top. I glared at her, thought briefly about delivering a jab to the ribs or maybe an uppercut to the chin. But then I remembered I was at work and in uniform. Besides, she looked like the type who might whup my ass and live to laugh about it. Instead of throwing punches, I threw a look and retreated to the rear of the aircraft.

Unfortunately, my escape was blocked by a massive presence in the aisle. It was the tipsy traveler. The big guy. The one who asked for *un vaso con hielo*. He stood there, wobbling, a sudden sense of purpose gleaming in his bloodshot eyes. Until that moment. I hadn't appreciated the mammoth proportions of the man. He stood well over six feet and weighed in at no less than three hundred pounds. Amid the shouts and screams of the escalating brawl, the big guy gathered his considerable voice and yelled something in Spanish. Something cruel and daunting and suicidal. He charged up the aisle, slamming into the fray with a fearlessness instilled by the makers of Barcardi. Had I not slid into a row of seats, he would have bowled me over like a cricket wicket.

The captain's voice soon came over the P.A. system, demanding that everyone be seated, but the escalating clamor made his command difficult to hear. Cheering sections had formed on the opposite side of the airplane. When a favorite brawler connected a punch, one group would yell "Whoooaaaaa" while the other group sighed "Ooooooh." From a protected position near the aft bulkhead, I watched an entire family— mother, father, and three kids—applauding and throwing phantom punches, like spectators at a Tyson fight. I'm certain

that in some hidden corner of the aircraft, someone was placing five-to-one odds on the big guy.

As law enforcement officers stormed the airplane, as
punches froze in mid-arc and pugilists suddenly became paci-
fists, the big guy moved to the back of the airplane and
looked me dead in the eye.

"Pssssst, pssssst..." he said, his eyes like wet tomatoes. "*Yo
necesito un vaso con hielo.* Ahhhh, ha, ha, ha, ha,..."

*Elliott Hester is a flight attendant, magazine writer, and newspaper
columnist. He is the author of* Plane Insanity: A Flight Attendant's
Tales of Sex, Rage and Queasiness at 30,000 Feet, *from which
this story was excerpted. He took a year off to travel the world and
is now living in Barcelona, Spain, while completing his second book,*
Adventures of a Continental Drifter.

* * *

I Am an Englishman

Wot was that you said?

AT JUST AFTER SEVEN-THIRTY WE WALKED INTO PAKISTAN. IT WAS like coming up for air. I rolled up my shirtsleeves for the first time in over a fortnight. Laura whooped, tore off her black headscarf, tossed her black stockings over the barbed wire, and danced a jig on her chador, to the delight of the Pakistani customs men. After the Iranians they seemed as unthreatening and familiar as Dixon of Dock Green. All around lay objects that I hadn't seen for three years, since I had left India. The customs officers sat on rope-strung charpoy, drinking little white china cups of milk-tea. Two sandalwood incense sticks were burning beside the immigration ledger. A bicycle leaned against the outside wall.

"What is your good name, sahib?" asked the customs officer, "and what is your mother country?"

I told him. They were the old familiar Indian questions. He took down a few more formal details.

"Are you wod?" he asked.

"What do you mean?"

9

"Are you and lady wod?"

"That's not English."

"You do not speak English, sahib?"

"I am English." There didn't seem any point in muddling the issue by bringing in Scotland.

"You have some words of English?"

"Yes, a number. I AM AN ENGLISHMAN."

This was an aspect of India that I had forgotten.

"Are you and lady wod?"

He made an obscene gesture with the first finger of his right hand.

"Wed! Do you mean are we wed?"

"Yes, are you and lady wod?"

"No." It was the first time we had admitted to not being married since Dogubayazit.

"Not wod?"

"NO I AM NOT WED."

"I am sorry, sahib. I am not understanding your English. I think perhaps that you are not speaking English good. Sahib, may I ask what is your mother tongue?"

"I've told you that. I am an Englishman and I speak English extremely well. Jesus Christ."

"Jesus?"

"He is calling on his God," explained the second customs officer.

"You are angry with me, sahib?"

"No, I am not angry with you, I just want to get on."

"Sahib, just one question."

"What?"

"You like bottom?" He pointed at me.

"I look like?"

"No, no sahib. You like bottom? I like bottom."

"I don't understand," I said. I really didn't

"Bottom, bottom," he said wiggling his head from side to side in the Indian manner. "I like bottom. I am bottom fan. You like bottom?"

"Well, I like some bottoms," I said.

"You do like bottom? You are bottom fan?"

"Yes."

"All English people like bottom."

"Oh yes," said the second customs official. "All Pakistani people like Imran Khan, all English people like Botham. He is your famous English cricketer."

William Dalrymple is author of numerous books, including City of Djinns, The Age of Kali, From the Holy Mountain, Lonely Planet Sacred India, *and* In Xanadu, *from which this story was excerpted. He is married to the artist Olivia Fraser, and divides his time between London, Edinburgh, and travels in the East.*

✵ ✷ ✵

The Snake Charmer of Guanacaste

There are strange things done under the tropical sun.

THERE'S ONLY ONE THING TO WORRY ABOUT IN COSTA RICA, and I was distressed to hear a woman screaming about it outside my bedroom door.

"*¡Culebra! ¡Culebra!*"

I threw off the covers and stumbled over to the door. When I opened it, there stood my neighbor, Mayela, hands clutched over her mouth.

"*¡Culebra!*" she gasped.

Spanish has two words for snake. The main one, *serpiente*, describes any kind of snake: garden snakes, sea snakes, big snakes, little snakes. Despite its ominous sound, the word *serpiente* doesn't alarm me. *Culebra* does.

A *culebra* is a poisonous snake. There are many kinds of *culebras* in the world, but on this remote coast there was just one: the fer-de-lance. I'd read in the newspaper of a local man who, while cleaning his garage, had moved a box and discovered a sleeping fer-de-lance. His wife found his corpse an hour later.

"*¿Donde?*" I asked Mayela.

"*¡Mira!*"

She pointed to a spot ten feet away, where the roof extended slightly from my little casita. In the overhang a coil of shiny scales glimmered in the sun. I rubbed the sleep from my eyes and squinted closer—yep, definitely a snake. Still groggy, I looked at Mayela, and chuckled.

Costa Rica is like the loveliest, and rarest, kind of woman: not only physically beautiful, but blessed with a miraculous internal stability. God graced her with natural beauty, from alluring shores to volcanic curves, but He kindly left out the political violence that plagues her Central American sisters. In 1890, Costa Rica held Latin America's first honest elections, and she's been a tropical democracy ever since. She's politically mature, but she's wonderfully wild, a land where you need not fear your fellow man but you must—as a matter of survival—fear the big-ass snakes.

Locals had warned me not to walk the countryside at night, lest I encounter a slithering predator on his midnight hunt. As it turned out, I hardly had to step outside my door to have the pleasure. While it was nice to get an up-close look at the local wildlife, I didn't fancy the prospect of coming home late at night—feeding time—and having to greet my new reptilian neighbor. I looked at Mayela.

"*¿Que hago?*" What should I do?

She looked at me and shrugged her shoulders.

"*Pues, tiene que matarla.*"

I had to kill it.

"*¿Con que?*"

"*Con un machete.*"

Had I been living in the United States, I might have balked. The American economy is so highly developed that we have professional "pest removers." All it takes is a phone call and a payment, and—poof!—snake problem solved. We've reached an unnerving level of advancement where a man can plop down on a bean-bag chair and, given a catheter and an Internet connection, never stand up again! This is why I left.

Nature did not design the young man to do a lot of sitting, but I had spent four years doing just that. My four years of college had been spent thinking lofty thoughts and doing absolutely nothing about them. No action; just sitting. Sitting in classrooms. Sitting in my bedroom. Sitting in the library. I had learned the minutiae of international economics and esoteric political theory, but oh, I was desperate to stand up. After four years of sitting down, I was desperate to leave behind comfort, pest professionals, and all those chairs, and to venture to a wild place, and to kill poisonous snakes by swinging a machete instead of writing a check.

I had a poisonous snake. Now I just needed a machete.

Machetes are like Central American credit cards—nobody leaves home without one. They're everywhere. The machete is part of the Central American male identity. The machete is the Swiss Army Knife on steroids, practicality manifest, the solution to every problem by which an American is rarely confronted: Need to hack a path through the jungle? Open a coconut? Kill a deadly reptile? The answer is a shining silver blade.

Ronnie, the self-proclaimed village womanizer, was burning palm fronds on the road in front of his house.

"*¿Porque quiere mi machete?*" he asked, a half-smile creeping across his face. He wasn't used to giving his machete to gringos.

"*Culebra.*"

His eyes lit up. In the last decade the gringo invasion has begun in earnest in Costa Rica, not just to visit but to settle, and they've even reached this tiny corner of Guanacaste on the northwest coast. The gringos enjoy an elevated place in society, mostly due to the fact that they have a lot of money. The few hotels are owned by gringos. The tourists here are gringos. Gringos are powerful. Wealthy. Educated. They don't dirty their hands; that's the labor of the locals. Ronnie was therefore delighted to see a gringo with a machete, psychologically preparing for battle with a fer-de-lance.

"Ha ha ha!" he cackled. *"¡Suerte! ¡Cuidado con esos diablos!"* Careful with those bastards!

I left Ronnie happier than I'd ever seen him, and walked through the field toward my casita in the tropical forest. I wrapped my hand around the cool black handle of the machete. I swung it around, chopping at imaginary beasts, the sharp steel slicing songs through the air.

"My friend!" greeted an English-speaking voice draped in an Eastern European accent. "Where you go?"

It was Yuri.

Every neighborhood has their six-foot, eight-inch alcoholic Russian bodybuilder; Yuri was ours. I had never really known him, which was entirely deliberate on my part. The low-down on Yuri was that he liked cheap wine, weight lifting, and philosophy. From what I'd heard, he usually did all three, all day, all at the same time.

I'd heard Yuri was a black hole of conversation—if you got sucked in, you weren't coming back out. If you had especially bad karma, Yuri would pull out his guitar and inflict his art. He claimed to have made an album once, "From Russia, With Love." Some speculated his ditties had once been a KGB torture method on political dissidents; but when *glasnost* devoured the Soviet Union, Yuri was out of a job and moved to Costa Rica to start his own hotel.

Yuri had indeed built his own hotel; single-handedly. He never hired a contractor, an electrician, a plumber, any machinery, and he never hired a single worker. This Russian giant had lifted every cinder block into place with his own Herculean hands. He had constructed a hotel. Alone. And it showed.

The Hotel Yuri was a big cinderblock shoebox. I think there were two stories, though I never found a staircase or any method whatsoever of reaching the second floor. An inexcusably polite person would have called the architecture "rustic." It reminded me of depictions of the Neolithic era in my sixth-grade science textbook—early man building his first shelter from the elements. The Hotel Yuri was like a historical theme park where I could step back in time and see the conditions in which Cro-Magnon man suffered. And Yuri was the resident Cro-Magnon.

I don't recall ever seeing a single guest at the Hotel Yuri. I would pass it daily, and no, never any guests—just Yuri, sitting in a chair, feet resting on a round plastic table, drinking wine.

The amenities of the Hotel Yuri were unparalleled. Rather, the amenity was unparalleled, for there was only one—and its credentials were dubious. The hand-painted sign (painted by Yuri) for Hotel Yuri boasted the enticing *Parque de Agua*—a waterpark. It consisted of a swimming pool, handcrafted by guess who? Yuri had splurged with the final touch: he had imported a toddler's slide from the town of Nicoya, a forty-five-minute drive, and positioned it next to the pool. The slide looked as though anyone over eight years old daring to brave its thrills would crush the jewel of the Hotel Yuri.

A local kid once told me he had been relaxing with his girlfriend one evening in Yuri's pool. Drinking a little, chatting, enjoying the slow pace of the tropics. Yuri was bench-pressing next to the pool, interspersing conversation between reps and grunts. Suddenly, he sat up. He scurried into the storage shed and returned with a jug of bleach. He began pouring liberal amounts into the pool, all around the local couple. They screamed in panic, as one would when doused in poison, but Yuri reassured them with calming gestures.

"Safe! Safe! Non-toxic!"

Yuri was something of a legend among the locals (who are generally small), a sort of cross between Sasquatch and Schwarzenegger.

"Come! Sit!" Yuri beckoned to me.

I'd been confronted by similar propositions from Yuri before, but always politely declined. But today was different. Today I was really experiencing the whimsical delights of Costa Rica, accepting and savoring its flavors, and I was more than happy to delay my task ahead.

"Sit, be comfortable, be happy." He nodded to an empty chair. "Wine?"

Yuri reached down and produced a vintage of the finest wine, produced from the finest grapes, packaged in the finest cardboard box. It was then that I observed the chalice from which Yuri was drinking: a clear, plastic measuring cup. He placed a twin cup before me and filled it to the brim.

"That's better," he sighed, filling his own cup, then leaning back contentedly. Somehow the Russian weight lifter in his *parque de agua* mirrored Buddha sitting under his tree of enlightenment.

"Tell me," he said, looking into my soul, "how is the great mystery they call life?"

I looked around. His weight bench, supporting a bar stacked with weights, squatted like a constipated lumberjack, a surreal vinyl throne in the *parque de agua*. A razor-sharp machete sat in my lap, soon to kill a deadly snake. I was drinking wine from a measuring cup with Andre the Giant in the Costa Rican wilderness.

The great mystery they call life was hilarious.

"Life's good."

Yuri looked expectant. He wanted something dripping with more philosophical juice. I just nodded my head and lowered my wine to 2½ cups. And then I blinked—all I did was blink, and Yuri was suddenly in the midst of a diatribe on the ills of humanity.

"...Man questing for power is like dog chasing own tail. Never get it. Never happy. Never satisfied. Power equals illusion. Life is not about power." It was a suspicious thing to hear from a weight lifter. "The only truth, the only truth that is real and good...is love."

He paused for effect.

Costa Rica seemed the perfect place for this enlightened Russian pacifist. After disputed presidential elections in 1948, a civil war ensued that most countries would laugh about, lasting a paltry six weeks. But Costa Ricans don't have much stomach for war—the whole thing sickened them, so when it was over, they abolished the army. Just completely eliminated it. Her citizens abhor militarism to this very day, and like to point out they've produced *más maestros que soldados*— more teachers than soldiers. When the 1980s came and Central America exploded into a series of civil wars, instead of getting dragged in, Costa Rican president Oscar Arias Sanchez devised a grand peace plan for all of Central America. It ended the wars in Nicaragua and El Salvador, restored order to the isthmus, and gave Costa Rica its winner of the Nobel Peace Prize.

"Yes, it is true," Yuri continued. "I follow no man and no government. I am follower of one thing, and that, you see, is love."

He sighed. He refilled our glasses.

There were no pressing engagements as we sat there absorbing the sun. Everything in the world could wait, including the snake. For most of the world, time is like a river that meanders lazily along. The Italians say "*La dolce far niente*": It is sweet to do nothing. Nowhere is this more true than in Costa Rica, where doing nothing is doing something. Time is endless and enigmatic. Schedules melt away. Multi-tasking is a disease, not a talent. Perfect weather produces the happiest and most inefficient people in the world.

Americans are different—time is the most precious commodity of all, fleeting and irretrievable, and I suddenly realized that spending time with this bohemian bodybuilder was the equivalent of flushing mine down the toilet. Americans see time as units of production. Time is money! Time is a currency that can be spent, invested, and wasted. "Doesn't thou love life?" advised Ben Franklin, "Then do not squander time!"

A medieval engraving by Albrecht Dürer called *Knight, Death, and the Devil* depicts a stoic knight riding his horse, yet Death incarnate follows close behind, holding an hourglass, a symbol for man's limited time on earth. The sand in the hourglass is falling fast: time is passing. Death will soon smother the knight. An American may scale Everest or dive to the bottom of the sea, but like Dürer's knight, we are haunted, always, by a faintly ticking clock, ticking like a phantom a few steps behind. The clock is always ticking.

Enduring a thirty-minute soliloquy by Yuri, however, had made me much more comfortable with the idea of dying. "Thanks for the wine," I said, standing up. "I better get going; I have an appointment."

"Where? With who?" Yuri inquired, suddenly fascinated at the prospect of someone having something to do.

"With a snake next to my door. I'm going to kill it." I raised the machete. Yuri almost fell over backwards in his chair.

"No!"

"What?"

"No kill snake! Snakes very beautiful creatures!"

"I can't just leave it there. It's a fer-de-lance."

"No, no, no!" Yuri was standing now, shaking his blond hair. He was a big lion, king of the jungle, Mufasa pleading for one of his fellow children of the wild. "Snakes very nice creatures! Very friendly! Eat and kill bad creatures!"

"Bad creatures?"

"Pesky mice…pesky squirrels…pesky, pesky birds!"

"Yuri, what if it was outside your door?"

He paused thoughtfully. For a moment I thought he would concede.

"Snake is *no poisonous*," he stated very matter-of-factly.

"Snake *is* poisonous!"

"No. Snake *looks* poisonous, but is not."

"You haven't even seen the snake!"

Yuri started to respond, then hesitated. He furrowed his brow, as if tallying up all the points, weighing them judiciously in his mind.

"No matter. No poisonous," Yuri announced conclusively.

There was no point in debating the Incredible Hulk. I shook my head and started to turn up the road when Yuri held up his hand.

"Wait, I have plan!"

Ten minutes later, Yuri stood like an ogre in the forest out-side my cabin door. He squinted at the hollow under the roofing, at the sinister coil of scales. He shook his head.

"You are safe. Snake is friendly."

Phase One of Plan Yuri then went into action. He pulled out a pair of enormous welding gloves, slipping them on one at a time. Any plan involving Yuri and welding gloves was a cause for serious concern.

Phase Two was activated. Yuri produced a laminated plastic sheet from his back pocket. Bold letters at the top read: "Snakes of Costa Rica." A hundred miniature photographs depicted every *serpiente* and *culebra* in the land. Yuri held up the sheet, looking at the coiled snake, then back at the sheet.

"You see? She no is fer-de-lance. She is 'cat-eyed wran-gler.' No poisonous."

I looked at the cat-eyed wrangler on the sheet, then at the snake above our heads. They looked as similar as a cup of coffee and a nuclear warhead.

"That's not a cat-eyed wrangler."

"Cat-eyed wrangler," Yuri whispered pleasantly.

Phase Three began.

"I show you snake is friendly."

The snake was still sleeping, or pretending to, lulling us into a false sense of security, just like the villain at the end of a movie. It had coiled itself into a hundred knots. It was impossible to judge how big it was—anywhere between two and twelve feet. Surely it must have sensed the vibrations from Yuri's voice just a few feet away, but it remained aloof, mysterious, waiting…

Yuri jumped up and punched the snake.

A "plan" had hinted of some sort of strategy, some shred of

rational thought. Even Yuri, I had thought, could not have come up with a plan as catastrophic as this. But if nothing else, Yuri's plan at least boasted the element of surprise, because the snake never saw it coming.

Yuri's exclamation of "Shit!" was the first clue that punching the snake was a mistake. It hissed a wicked threat, uncoiled instantly, and tried to slither deeper into the hollow—away from this strange new creature, this giant punching Russian. But incredibly, the punching Russian creature pursued. He jumped up and down, trying again and again to grab it with those big, awkward gloves. I jumped back and readied the machete, waiting for the snake to lash out.

"Yuri, careful!"

Yuri grabbed the snake by the tail and held fast, leaving its head free to whip around. This was a living example of natural selection: the human race was better off without Yuri, so he was courteously about to remove himself from it.

"Come, come," he soothed the snake.

The tug of war between man and beast ended when Yuri leaped and gave the snake's tail an almighty yank, and down the *culebra* came. Now Yuri was holding a furious snake, writhing in the air. It undulated like sea swells, hissing, raging, trying to slither away.

"Beautiful creature," Yuri admired.

The beautiful creature raised its head, bared its two needle fangs, and sent them speeding toward Yuri. It was a National Geographic special gone horribly wrong. It was a cobra attacking the snake-charmer before a stunned crowd. It was the wrath of savage nature against an ignorant man.

Those gloves, those industrial welding gloves, likely born for the hellish heat of some Soviet factory deep in the core of Stavropol or Kiev, where men wore metal masks reflecting sparks and magma, those gloves that proved impenetrable to the magma of Stalin's industrial obsession, his drive to transform the fatherland into a place of iron and fire, proved a match for the teeth of a tropical snake. Those gloves saved Yuri's life. The snake buried its fangs into them, and they were now stuck there. The snake shook back and forth, trying to free itself, but it was useless.

"Hello, beautiful creature," Yuri cooed.

Beautiful creature, its fangs rendered useless, now began wrapping its scaly body around Yuri's arm, squeezing like a boa constrictor.

"Oh, strong creature." Yuri smiled.

Strong creature continued to squeeze until it had completely wrapped itself around the great Russian arm. Strong creature was a good six feet long.

"Yuri, that thing's poison! Grab its head and we'll bring it to Rancho Diablo and they'll tell you."

This made sense to Yuri. The rancho was a little surf camp under construction, 500 yards away, and there were always six or eight locals working on it. They would know, the men who grew up here and knew everything about Guanacaste, its tides and moons, its storms and its predators. The locals at Rancho Diablo were like the Supreme Court, and their judgment was sound. They would, Yuri reasoned, confirm the snake's innocence and let him go free.

So we set off down the dirt road to the Devil's Ranch, the bodybuilder in welding gloves, a huge snake coiled around his left arm, the "Snakes of Costa Rica" chart in his right. His glance shifted back and forth between the two, as if he was trying to come to a very important decision—which, of course, he was. His giant shirtless frame rippled with muscle and reflected the mid-morning sun. His flip-flops shuffled along, stirring little clouds of sun-baked dirt. The air was shining with the clear smell of sun and sea. The palms fronds whispered above like a rolling river. Somehow, everything was normal. This was life in Guanacaste. There were no schedules, so there was nothing to be distracted from, and when something unexpected arose, it was no surprise. One just accepted whatever happened to come along, be it a hurricane or a poison snake wrapped around the arm of an expatriate Russian. As I walked a safe distance from Yuri and the snake, I breathed easy and wore a tickled smile because this was not America, and I was not sitting down.

The men at Rancho Diablo were on a work break. They sat on the grass in a semi-circle before the half-built house, some snacking on fruit, none of them even vaguely familiar with work-related stress—and only slightly familiar with work, really. All of them had mustaches and machetes, the two prerequisites for a rural Central American man. A few wore American baseball caps. They looked up when Yuri walked into their circle.

He never even had a chance to ask.

They jumped up and backed away, pointing at the serpent on Yuri's arm.

"¡Culebra! ¡Culebra!"

The scene was like an old Western, when two notorious gunslingers exchange insults in a saloon and the rest of the clientele runs for cover in a mad shoving about of tables and chairs.

"Pero no es culebra," Yuri explained. *"No tiene veneno."*

"¡Si, tiene veneno!"

"¡Matelo!"

"¿Que diablos esta haciendo?"

"¡Es culebra!"

Yuri shook his head, a little less confidently, a hint of dread in his voice. "*Es un* 'cat-eyed wrangler.' *¿Sí? ¿No?*"

He even waved around the laminated "Snakes of Costa Rica" as proof, but nobody was paying attention. Their eyes were fixed on the real thing.

Something in Yuri's expression wavered. He looked at the men around him, all staring intently at the thing coiled around his right arm. And with a sigh of profound resignation, as though wishing he was somewhere very, very far away from that arm, the fact penetrated his brain: he was holding a fer-de-lance.

He smiled uncomfortably. He looked around for some assistance, but none was forthcoming.

Yuri, it turned out, had more conviction than I thought. The Costa Ricans were shouting to kill the snake. But Yuri, even though he was clearly a little worried, would have none of it. He just shook his head.

"Snake beautiful creature," he insisted. "I let live."

Yuri was a lover of humanity, of life, and even of poisonous snakes; Yuri would not kill the beautiful creature, who somehow began to lose its monstrous qualities and take on the look of a scared prisoner. The snake had committed no crime other than living near a man, and now a group of men were calling for its execution. An hour earlier, the snake was a villain. Now it was a victim, and Yuri, the only man in danger, was the only man defending it. He lifted his free hand to silence the cries of the men.

"Snake deserve freedom, not death."

He walked across the dirt road to the edge of the forest. He kneeled down, holding the snake firmly by its triangular head, and he pulled its fangs free from the gloves. The locals watched this whole process quietly, as it defied logic, as did everything with Yuri. I looked at the speechless Costa Ricans and imagined them, thirty years from now, sitting in a dark tavern and reminiscing over a quickly disappearing bottle of *guarro*. "Do you remember that morning," one of them would say, "when the gringo *grande* saved the *culebra*?" And they would laugh and shake their heads incredulously, fondly re-calling the legend of the snake-charmer of Guanacaste to anyone who wasn't there. I felt a certain privilege to witness this legendary feat of the Russian giant, what certainly must have been Yuri's induction into the annals of local folklore.

Still kneeling, Yuri unraveled the *culebra*, all six feet of it, from his arm and held its great body with an ease that no normal human could have. He tossed its head first and released the body an instant later, a gentle toss that sent the serpent onto the forest floor.

It slithered away, gliding over roots and around trees, into the crystal sphere of forest whose ancient trees stood like pillars that held the sky aloft. The sun cascaded down and filtered through the leaves, glimmering and winking like can-dles in the shade. A thousand unseen birds warbled and chirped. A cool breath of breeze swayed the green vines and brown branches. The smell of the elements, of virgin earth, permeated the air. The snake was almost invisible now, becoming smaller and smaller, as it camouflaged back into its wild domain.

There is only one thing to worry about in Costa Rica, and that problem was now solved, at least for the time being. There was nothing to do but inhale deeply and smile in the tropical sun. Like the loveliest, and rarest, of women, Costa Rica has a magical way of making problems melt away. In this land of alluring coves and volcanic curves, home to giant Russians and poisonous snakes, the nearest ticking clock seemed a thousand miles away.

Patrick Fitzhugh created the CD "Sailors, Whalers, and Witches,"
a narrated travel guide through Cape Cod's mist-shrouded past.
He has sung karaoke in Nicaragua, been stranded in Sarajevo, arm-
wrestled in Mexico, lost a drinking competition in Guatemala, and
eaten Cocoa Puffs in Romania. He currently works with boats at
an unnamed Pacific port.

* * *

Good Dog!

What was that sound in the night?

As a new Peace Corps volunteer in a village in Mali, West Africa, I was prepared for any calamity that could come my way. I was ready for snakes, scorpions, malaria, motorcycle accidents, and countless parasitic intestinal guests. Bring it on! All of these, plus a number of other unanticipated challenges, were hurled my way in two years of living in the village of Kangaba. Yes, I was fresh out of college, and ready for my AFRICAN ADVENTURE. I liked to think of it in all caps, just like in *A Prayer for Owen Meany*. That way, it was sure to be significant.

About three months into my service, I had adjusted to eating millet every night (you know it more affectionately as "birdseed"); squatting over a pit toilet with the cockroaches; eating goat innards with my hands out of the community bowl with my host family; working hard in the fields all day, and not speaking English for weeks at a time. All this, I thought, would impress the folks back home and was not really such a big deal, because I felt so at home already with my friends in the village.

One night, as usual, I was reading in bed in my mud hut, under a mosquito net. I was also taking care of a dog that belonged to another volunteer while he was away from the village traveling. The dog, Che, was a medium-sized plain Black Lab type of dog. Not the sharpest arrow in the quiver, but a faithful companion, and I liked having him around. Each night, I would take my eyeglasses off (I don't need them for reading), put them on the bedside table, grab my book, and tuck myself into the mosquito net, armed only with a fifty-cent flashlight from the local market. Ah, I was all tucked under my net like a cocoon, reading a well-worn, yellow-paged Barbara Kingsolver book that had lovingly been passed from volunteer to volunteer. I was remembering that in the height of the Malian empire, books traded for more than gold in Timbuktu, and I thought of history repeating itself among the Peace Corps diaspora. We loved books.

I suddenly became distracted by Che's actions. He had been lying next to my bamboo bed quite contentedly. I sat up to observe him, with foggy focus because my glasses were outside the mosquito net. He was standing at attention with perky ears, body in geometrically perfect alignment, one paw raised straight. It was pointing toward an area right underneath my bottom, under the bed. *Hmmmm…*I thought. *I guess there is another mouse, or a lizard under there. Ah, well, back to the book.* I dismissed Che like an underpaid lackey.

But Che was still pointing, like an English hunting dog, and I wondered admiringly where he had learned that trick. I decided to slowly pull the straw mattress back, so I could peek under the bed frame and scare the mystery critter out. As I peered about four inches under my precious buttocks, I saw a very large, beady-eyed, not-very-friendly looking rat the size of a camel. Like me, the rat became startled, Che became consumed by instinct, and my heart hammered against my ribs at an alarming rate. After that, as they say, it was all a blur. Literally. My glasses were still *outside* the mosquito net on the table, and I could not see beyond the distance of a book. I was too terrified to risk putting a limb out of my cocoon. I shook my flashlight, cursing the faltering life span of the batteries. The weak golden glow emanating from the cheap plastic torch was illuminating just enough of the drama in front of me to keep me curled up fetus-tight, protecting my buttocks and other extremities, my heart pounding.

I heard pig-like squeals, wolf-like growls, baby-like cries, and Hitchcockian screams. The two producers of this cacophony made their way to the corner of my bedroom, over to my makeshift concrete-block shelves in the corner. Whoa! There went three pair of underwear and a few pairs of socks, airborne over the rat-dog cyclone below. I squinted to see more of what was going on, and I caught a blurry glimpse of a small stuffed teddy bear, dressed in a lacy smock my mother had sent me in a recent care package. *How embarrassing that she did that to her twenty-three-year-old hippie daughter*, I thought at the time. But now that Teddy was turning to shreds as it did acrobatics in the air above the scuffle, I became enraged at the rat for violating a symbol of love from my mom so far away. I was pissed. "Go, Che!" I cheered like a WWF wrestling fan. The screeches grew louder, undergarments still flying in the air. I was still squinting, and my hands clenched harder on the flashlight as it sputtered and ran out of juice.

Darkness. Silence. I waited, hearing my own accelerated breath. I heard Che's paws on the concrete floor coming closer to me. Courageously reaching a hand outside the mosquito net, I retrieved my lantern and eyeglasses. I struck the match to inspect the aftermath. O.K., my Peace Corps recruiter did not tell me about nights like this. My bedroom was a disaster area! Torn-up underwear and socks, a de-stuffed, de-smocked, de-headed teddy bear, and rat blood in puddles all over the floor.

Meanwhile, Che, all of a sudden, was a proud, A+ student who had just completed his final exam of Smart Dog Academy. The limp, lifeless rat at my feet was the assessment. He looked at me, begging for praise, and hoping for some sort of treat for his efforts. "Yeah, that's just frickin' great," I heard myself say out loud to him. "Good job. Now get that thing out of here! Out, out!" He was all of a sudden dunce dog again. He laid it closer to my feet and smiled a stupid smile. I think he drooled on purpose. "Arrrrrgggh!" I marched to the next room and got inventive. I returned with my rudimentary garden hoe and the dustpan. I scooped the rat up, tossed him into the dark yard for now, and returned to mop up the blood-soaked teddy-bear stuffing.

As I was cleaning the room, thinking what-an-independent-strong-adventurous-woman-I-am-and-I'm-in the-middle-of-Africa-in-the-middle-of-the-night-all-by-myself-and-I'm-just-fine-cleaning-up-rat-blood, no-problem, I-am made-for-this-kind-of-challenge, but-I'm-getting-a-little-lump-in-my-throat, Che came *back* inside. He was portering the limp rat, and laid it at my feet as if to say, "I don't think you had your glasses on last time, so maybe you didn't see what a good boy I am." I noted the size of the rat. Big. I took a deep breath, patted his head, and tried to be sincere. "Good boy, Che." I tossed him a hunk of stale bread, and he happily trotted to the corner. I chucked the rat outside again, and locked the door.

Somehow, I managed to clean up the room, put away some non-shredded clothes that survived the battle, have a good little homesick sniffle about the teddy bear, wash my hands about ten times, then curl back up with my book. I kept my glasses nearby this time. I slept well.

The next morning, I realized the rat did not just vaporize into rat heaven, and it was squarely in my path on the way to the cockroach-inhabited latrine. *Hmmm*…I went over to my host family's hut across the dirt path from my hut for a much-needed intervention. I was surprised how much Bambara I knew, and couldn't believe I had acquired the vocabulary to explain the night's events satisfactorily to my host family's comprehension. I felt quite proud for a moment. They asked me if I was O.K., had a little laugh at my expense, then sent one of the older brothers over to my yard to take care of the rat.

Now, this older brother seemed from time to time to delight in shocking the new, naïve, *toubab* woman. This was one of those times. As he reached down to pick up the rat, he said casually, "Lunch."

"Lunch?" I choked out. I wanted to be sure I understood his Bambara. I eat lunch with the family every day.

He made sure to make eye contact with me, which is rare for gentle Malians. He locked onto my eyes and said essentially, "Yup, and this is the best part." He held up the rat corpse, yanked off the testicles and held them up in his palm for me to see. I smiled back, trying as hard as ever not to show the complete horror I was sure was all over my face.

"Well, then, *bon appetit*," I said, and sent him on his way.

I stood there for a minute in my hot, dusty yard in Kangaba, Mali, where I felt so strangely at home, trying to figure out what lesson, what great meaning this event could bring to my life. I was feeling very sure that something profound was happening out of all this.

But then I shrugged my shoulders and strolled over towards my hammock to take a nap before lunch. "If it's not a good time, it's a good story," I told myself. That would be my mantra for the rest of the two years I lived in Mali, which were, absolutely, the most profound and magical years of my life.

Mary Noble got hooked on travel during her time living in Africa. She currently teaches at an international school in Thailand and spends summers in Alaska and Michigan. This is her first published story! If you want to send her advice about not using mixed metaphors, you can reach her at mary_noble@hotmail.com.

* * *

Disturbing the Peace

Who do you turn to when you hear voices in the night?

CLOUDS FALL OVER THE SLEEPY VILLAGE OF SANTA ELENA, Costa Rica as the chirping birds sing in the sweet symphony of the night. The occasional monkey howls off in the distance as the wind rustles the leaves and branches throughout the forest. Nestled in their beds, the villagers sleep off a hard day's work of rebuilding the central plaza.

The silence of the night is suddenly shattered by a commotion in a dark hostel. At the top of his lungs, a man is screaming "Help me!" in Spanish and English. It sounds like he is beating the walls. The screams echo throughout the night as men emerge from their houses and follow the screams to the hostel. A small group of bleary-eyed travelers point to room number 5. They knock, but no one answers.

I didn't hear a thing.

One year later and thousands of miles away, a hostel in Buenos Aires is tormented by an angry voice that screams throughout the night. A German awakens in his top bunk to find a bearded man staring him right in the face. The bearded man starts to scream and ask crazy questions. He wants directions to Brazil and wants to know if someone mowed his mother's lawn. "Be careful, there's pirates out there," he says as he points to the wall. The awakened travelers stare in confusion as he slowly returns to his bed in a peaceful sleep. The next day, they ask to change rooms.

I didn't hear a thing.

Deep in the Amazon Basin, a group of men snore in their hammocks as a misty rain beats down upon them. The chirping insects slowly give way to a human-like growl. The men wake to loud talking off in the blackness of the jungle. But there is something wrong: they hear only one voice. The voice grows louder, ending in a final scream and then stops as a ruckus erupts in the bushes. The chirping of the insects takes over again as one of the men grabs his machete and goes to investigate. Other than a man sleeping quietly in his hammock, he finds nothing.

I didn't hear a thing.

A cold breeze blows over the small island of Isla Taquille. Nestled in the blue waters of Lake Titicaca, it is secluded from the modern world. An old man is sleeping on a mat in his adobe house. A faint knocking on the wall wakes him. Every few minutes it stops, as he hears a rustling on the dirt floor. He starts to hear voices. The footsteps sound like something is walking around in circles in the room next to him. Peering out the window, he finds an enormous, candlelit man staring right at him.

I didn't hear a thing.

It's four A.M., somewhere in Central Mexico. A ramshackle bus travels the dark, desert highways on its way to the United States. On board, the humming of the engine is interrupted by the occasional snore of the sleeping passengers. In the darkness of the vehicle, a voice starts speaking in English. But no one is responding. One by one, the passengers wake. Flicking their lighters, they look through the pile of sleeping bodies on the floor to find a gringo lying on his side. His head is resting on an old shirt as his open eyes stare at the wall of the bus. He's having a conversation with something underneath the seat. As the men bend to look, small children begin to cry. It's scaring them.

The entire bus wakes to the shouting as one man stands over the gringo and looks into his face. He continues to shout at the wall. The man squats down to look underneath the seat but finds nothing. Standing up to face the worried passengers he shouts, "The gringo is crazy!"

With a drool-covered face, I wake to a busload of laughing Mexicans. I stand up to see their dimly lit faces staring at me, and I wonder just what is so funny. "Can you introduce us to your friend under the seat?" someone shouts from the darkness.

I always had a suspicion that I was the one causing the trouble.

It is a strange feeling to wake up and find your room trashed—but the door still locked. Or, you wake up on the floor beside your bed. You might even wake up to find all of your bags unpacked. But it's the worst when you emerge from hammocks, hostels, and overnight buses to a crowd of curious stares and half-hidden smiles. You hear the whispering, see the smiling faces and pointing fingers. Locals and travelers alike become afraid of you. "If he is that violent in his sleep, imagine what he might do when he is awake?" they say.

Over my travels, I have developed a habit of starting every day by apologizing for the night before.

⋆

Craig D. Guillot would like to apologize sincerely to all the locals and travelers whom he has scared and aggravated. From now on, he promises to avoid hostels and sleep only in the most secluded places, far from shouting distance.

JONO MARCUS

* * *

It's Dar es Salaam and I Am Not Dead

Getting robbed was the good part.

I AM ON A TRIP FROM MOMBASA, KENYA TO DAR ES SALAAM, Tanzania, the overnight bus timely, in an African sort of way, in its three-hour retarded departure. En route, smooth Kenyan roads gradually turn Tanzanian, torn and potholed from the second world war. The bus isn't full, so Caleb and I commandeer two sets of back seats for the long night ahead. We gradually learn to tie our waists to the seats with webbing from our packs and lock our arms underneath only to endure one hellish bounce after another, each jolt punching our bodies a second before dreams take us.

Caleb is the archetypal robust Australian, the kind of guy who hikes through wet mountain brush in sneakers lined with plastic bags. He knows the names of every species of insect that come across our East African path and befriends everyone we meet, even the police who continually stop unaccustomed tourists with the intention of extorting them. Those proud police inevitably end up buying us drinks at their local bar instead because Caleb's charm turns corrupt police into our new best friends.

In Dar es Salaam, Caleb and I find a simple guest house near the city center, the Hotel Mbowe, which overlooks a depressing though colorful city. Neon signs for Coca-Cola and Kodak cover the buildings, yet the pervasive hot African wind blows street dirt throughout, caking our sweat with muddy grease. At our first dinner in Dar, a thinly robed man swears at us for being underdressed, exclaiming that our dirty tank tops, torn shorts, and sandals should be white-collared shirts, ties, slacks, and shiny black shoes. He insists that we, as white men, have a responsibility to Black Africa to dress smartly. Our argument with him lasts deep into the slimy night, gradually leaning towards a brawl as he drinks bottle after bottle of Tusker lager.

Five days in Dar and we find few redeeming qualities. Flies everywhere buzz around food stalls; disease seems to run rampant like the wild dogs which, around dusk each day, attempt to corner us in the precarious alleyway behind the Hotel Mbowe. They can have me at this point. I'm tired. I've been traveling on a shoestring for a year and can't continue any farther this way. I consider my return home: clean beds without those elusive yet omnipresent bed bugs, guaranteed fresh water, food prepared according to the laws of science, free of worms. Or I could travel farther south to Zambia on the Tazara railway, a path laid with malaria, yellow fever, and hepatitis; mysterious hivers, strange and exotic mumpers, all caused by some weird tropical insect whose name Caleb will know but whose effects he may not be able to alleviate. I'm tired of watching my bags, watching for muggers, watching for danger, searching for the cheapest way to travel, the cheapest place to stay, the cheapest way to eat. I am bored, fed up, and annoyed when I notice that I am missing $300 from my passport pouch.

These are the days when hard currency must be declared upon entering the country. To dissuade tourists from exchanging money on the black market, Tanzania enforces strict currency regulations. When tourists enter the country, they record all the money they have on a currency declaration form. When you exchange your money, you do so at government banks where you get stamps on your currency declaration form proving you exchanged your money there. When you leave, you again declare and record the money you have left. The amount you arrive with minus the amount you exchange at the government banks should be the amount of money you have when you leave.

When the border police do the math and find $300 missing, I can be detained, arrested, or worse. I heard a horrific tale from a worn Dutch traveler in Mombasa who had lost money too and reported that fact to the Tanzanian police. The police, believing he had exchanged the money on the black market, locked him up and slapped him around for twelve days before he bribed his way out of jail for five hundred dollars.

"Each day I was in the jail, they raised the amount of the bribe. It started at a hundred dollars and I thought they were crazy to think I would pay it. I told them this and waited for the court date to come. I knew that after a week the court date was never going to come."

I thought of this ragged Dutch guy when making the decision whether or not to report my stolen money to the police. Do I run the risk of being searched, discovered, and detained at the Zambian border (which I heard was a very rough crossing for travelers) or do I run the risk of being arrested, detained, and perhaps beaten if I go to the police here in Dar es Salaam?

I decide that I should go to the Tanzanian police here in Dar and take my chances when two brothers, Joseph and Joseph (same father, different mothers, they assure me) harmlessly walk with me and ask questions about my travels.

"Friend, where are you from?" Joseph #1 asks.

"USA." I reply, watching their hands in case they want to take my money, my passport, my camera. Such is the second nature for the Third World traveler, being on constant watch to guard his or her very few valuables, while maintaining a polite, friendly demeanor.

"Friend, have you been in Tanzania a long time?" the brother of Joseph asks. Both of these men are lean, stringy, with seven or eight teeth missing between them. I decide I like them. They actually feel harmless.

"Not too long," I reply simply, with a little less distance.

"Where are you going?" the first Joseph asks. I stop with them on the sidewalk and decide to tell them my story. They are innocently inquisitive, soft and bony, a contrasting balm to the tough African street.

"I had some money stolen in Zanzibar and I need to report it to the police."

"Oh, no! You should not do that! You will be put in the jail. Police don't like it when tourists trade the money on the black market," Joseph exclaims. He seems to care about me. I am touched, surprised; I soften my stance one more degree.

"I didn't trade money on the black market but I have to go anyway. It's the right thing to do."

"You will get in big trouble if you do that. Let us help you instead."

I am so bored that I consider the possibility. I want something to mix me up just a little bit. When you are on the road a long time in Africa, you always think that you've heard it

all. In Malindi, Kenya, Caleb and I met a guy trying to sell us
Black Mercury. We imagined that Black Mercury was a code
word for Brown Sugar which was a code word for heroin, but
we had to ask. He said, "No man, not heroin, black mercury,
you know the stuff they put in thermometers, it's silver, but
then we dye it black."

Caleb and I, jaws open, passed on the Black Mercury, but
here in Dar I decide to give the brothers Joseph the opportunity to make a few bucks, so I ask them, "What do you have
in mind?"

Joseph and Joseph tell me their story as we sit at the
Salamander restaurant on smelly Samora Avenue.

"I will stay with you, while my brother Joseph takes your
currency form to his friend at the bank who will stamp the
form saying that you have exchanged $300 dollars, so there
will be no problems for you."

I think about it. It would reduce the risk of arrest, detain-
ment, or any unfortunate beatings at the border. I think again
about the worn Dutch traveler and the twelve days he spent
in prison.

"O.K. I don't know why I'm doing this, but here you go.
Take care with it and hurry back." I give him two dollars and
tell him he can have more if he comes back soon.

I order a *chai* for myself and a coffee for the other Joseph.
For fifteen minutes we talk about Dar and the Salamander
restaurant and his brother. The *chai* is very sweet, surprisingly
delicious. My new friend is nervous, his bony long legs
bouncing up and down like some American kid hooked on
Coca-Cola.

"Relax," I tell him. "Everything will be fine." I convince
myself that this is also true before Joseph returns and says that
there was some "trouble."

He mumbles into my ear, "The police found us, they are outside waiting." I follow him out to the street where four men surround me and hold me, tell me to get into the car.

"My mother always told me not to get into the car with strangers." I actually say this, trying to lighten the severity of the situation when they show me their police badges. I acquiesce and they gruffly push me into their car.

It all happens so fast. The last thing I remember is the face of a white woman traveler who looks at me with such a maternally sad and helpless face that I imagine it's the last face I'll ever see. This is my fate, I relinquish. I am going to be beaten, locked up, then beaten again.

We drive around Dar es Salaam in silence for ten minutes, two short policemen in front, one of them driving. From the back they look angry, their necks tight, their ligaments straining through their skin. Joseph, I, and Joseph in that order sit crushed in the back seat, all of their legs on either side of me bouncing up and down, giving me different looks. On one side, Joseph gives me that "don't worry everything is going to be O.K." look. That side is comforting. On the other side, Joseph gives me that "we are all going to die" look. That side I don't like so much but I am stuck somewhere in the middle. When I am about to ask what's going to happen, the policeman in the passenger side suddenly spins around and lifts a wooden stick above his head threatening to bash our collective brains, then speaks in English while I, in shock, imagine my crushed skull in my hands.

"You stupid tourist! Did you think you get away with it? What person are you, you challenge the authority of the government of Tanzania? We work the country to help people and you come with your America and your money and think you buy anything. Our money is weak to yours so strong but you betray our country, our people, and you trade your dollar on the black market."

He yells something at the brothers Joseph in Swahili and they dart glances at each other. We are all going to jail. We are all going to be beaten.

I begin to speak, "But, that's not what…" He lifts the wooden stick again and check swings it at me.

I flinch and shut up.

Joseph on one side assures me, his hand on my knee, "Be calm, everything is going to be O.K., they won't hurt you," and on the other side, Joseph scares me with "You better watch what you say to these men, they hurt you bad, don't lie to them."

We drive by one of the newer buildings on the block, a sign in front saying something in Swahili. The man in front turns and speaks again,

"You see that building, that is prison. We lock you up, criminals there. That is where you go. We lock you up and throw away the key because you break our law. We lock you up, beat you and leave you to die."

I have a chance to see his face with less confusion. He has a leaden brow, a face in knots. His whole head looks like a frayed rope with the edge burnt off. His shirt is wet from sweat, it sticks to his body and his black skin shades his white collared shirt brown.

Joseph turns to me softly, holding my arm. "Don't worry, *rafiki*," he silently pleads to me, his friend. His brother, Joseph, turns to me also just after his brother speaks and says frantically, "Just do whatever he wants and you won't be hurt." They are in stereo, left speaker assuring me, right speaker freaking me out. It's like some tripped out tune from Pink Floyd's *Dark Side of the Moon*.

We drive away from the prison for the second time and I don't know what they are going to do to me. I am afraid, and I feel something important is happening somewhere else, like my guardian angel up in heaven is making phone calls, wheeling deals, trading out future options for immediate investment.

"The money, I swear, it was stolen and I was afraid to go to the police. I am sorry, I swear I am sorry, in Zanzibar, at the guest house…" I say.

I find myself pleading with the brothers instead. The brothers, long-faced, look through me at each other with sincere helplessness. I feel a hole opening beneath me; the severe, tight-faced man in the front seat with the big wooden stick decides my fate, whether he will beat my skull or lock me up to watch me whither away. I imagine worse for the brothers Joseph. East Africans have been known to bludgeon other East African criminals to death. I'd rather not think what is in store for them.

"Lies! All lies! We are no fools! No. We see your kind before. We see people like you come to our country, trade money in the black market and we arrest you and lock you up and beat you and throw away the key. You no different, you are like the rest. You tourists all think you are better than Tanzania. Your capitalism cheats us, just like you cheat us." Again, harsh words to the Josephs in Swahili. Again darting glances.

The car is silent as we wait at a traffic light. A chicken runs past the front of the car, a small black child running after it. Should I try to get out? On either side of me is Joseph and Joseph. Should I beg? Should I offer them money? We drive by the prison again, the knotted grunt up front spins around and almost strikes me in the face with the stick. I don't see it coming because I am watching the boy chasing the chicken, thinking of the portent—the boy will catch the chicken in some alleyway where he will find my broken body. When the stick grazes within an inch of my otherwise occupied mind, both Josephs flinch for me and grab my arms. That scares me more than the waving stick and I jump. The car turns into an alley heaped with garbage, the hard sun finding no place to rest between two decaying buildings. Here it comes. This is it. I see that same ominous chicken, but the boy is nowhere to be found. I better think of something fast. I am about to be beaten repeatedly in the head with a big wooden stick in Dar es Salaam, Tanzania. The chicken pecks at a dried apple core.

"Do you want to die in a prison cell?"

"No," I nervously answer.

"Do you want we lock you up and beat you?"

"No."

"Do you want us to arrest you."

"No." I answer again.

"Then you give us three hundred dollars."

The skinny is out. I get it now. I know that I have that much in cash and in travelers' checks and I see a flint of sunshine at the end of the alleyway. I am going to buy my way out of this mess and I am grateful that I have the money and it gives me a little tingly feeling that I am not going to be arrested, locked up, beaten, killed. The chicken lets out a "car-r-r-aww," when I see the grunt's face clearly a second time. He wants the money and he wants to end this ride. I can't believe how his face has changed. I am less scared, but perhaps I shouldn't be.

"But I just had three hundred dollars stolen from me," I whine and begin to bargain for position, "and that would mean I lose six hundred dollars and how am I going to explain that to the border police?"

He raises the stick, looks at it, doesn't swing. I re-evaluate my position.

I explain, "I don't have that much in cash, but I can give you travelers' checks instead. That's all I have."

The policeman in front looks to the driver who nods, then looks to Joseph and Joseph who also nod. Joseph and Joseph nod. Their approval. They nod. I can't believe it. They are in on the deal too. Joseph and Joseph, brothers, what the hell was I thinking? They all agree on the travelers' checks and I carefully take out fifteen twenties in American Express travelers' checks, count them out and sign them off to Joseph, the comforting one, who receives the checks with a shallow grin.

I ask them to drop me off at the Hotel Mbowe. I don't know why I become so cocky all of a sudden, perhaps because I realize that all they ever wanted from me was the money and I am mad at Joseph, both of them. They drop me off at my hotel. When I get out, I see the car they are driving is a taxi cab. Funny, I think, why would policemen drive around in a taxi cab? Must be some undercover operation.

I am visibly carrying the smell of fear. Caleb smells it and is quiet for the seven or eight seconds it takes me to say, "I think I was just mugged."

"Tell me what happened," he says to me, slowly sitting me down. I am getting scared because I can see in his eyes that I am shaking. I tell him about the boredom and the brothers Joseph and the Salamander restaurant and the friend in the bank and the cops and the drive and the prison and the big wooden stick. I tell him about the political speeches and the story of the Dutch traveler and the big wooden stick. I tell him about the travelers' checks and the counting and the big wooden stick. I am frazzled and panicked and he says, "Get your passport, we're going to the American embassy."

After the near miss of being arrested, locked up, beaten, and left to die, the vision of a massive, solid, corn-fed marine in fatigues with an M-16 is a welcome sight. I thank God and bless the United States of America. When I walk in, the marine doesn't move but acknowledges us with his eyes. He lets us in. I am an American and he is an American and Caleb and I are safe.

We meet with Barbara Johnson, a strict and untrusting woman who hears our story. I tell her all about the money stolen in Zanzibar and the two men who take my currency declaration form. (I don't tell her that their names were Joseph and Joseph or that they were brothers.) I tell her about the Salamander restaurant on Samora Avenue and the police badges and the taxi cab and the ride and the prison and the big wooden stick and the political speeches and the travelers' checks and all of it.

She asks me blankly, "Why do you guys trade on the black market when the U.S. dollar is worth so much?"

I can't believe it. I respond politely, "I didn't. I swear. It was stolen in Zanzibar and…"

"Look, it doesn't matter. Let's first get you a refund on your travelers' checks." She calls American Express and I get an immediate refund for my travelers' checks. She makes another call while we wait outside her office, then calls us in and says to me, "You are very lucky. Those men weren't policemen. Policemen don't bait tourists like that and they don't drive around in taxi cabs. Something like this happened three weeks ago on the outskirts of the city. Men posing as police with fake badges picked up a tourist, blackmailed him, then beat him severely with a wooden stick. He came within an inch of death. You lost three hundred dollars, but you escaped with your life."

Could it be the same wooden stick? I sat in her office for ten minutes not hearing her and Caleb talk about the next step. I was lost for the briefest moment, then in an instant, I resolutely decided to continue on the African road rather than return home. I was almost killed! I was almost beaten to a bloody pulp with a raging wooden stick. I couldn't go home now, I owed too much on my East African karma credit plan and my guardian angel worked so hard to save me that it would be an insult to return home. Damn the malaria! Damn the yellow fever! Damn the mysterious hivers and the strange and exotic mumpers! Damn the thieves and most of all damn that big wooden stick. And to think that I considered leaving these wandering roads for a more comfortable and secure life in the States! Forget that! I am a traveler and damned if I am going to let a near-death experience scare me away, turn me home when the rest of Africa awaits my weary legs and unyielding eye.

Barbara Johnson notices I am not paying attention and interrupts my euphoria, "You must go to the police station for real this time, no funny business. Go there and tell them exactly what you told me."

I chime in, a reconfirmed citizen of the East African road, "But I heard they detain people, especially travelers who travel on the cheap because they think that we all exchange our money on the black market."

"That's because you all do exchange your money on the black market. But if they detain you in any way take this number."

She gives Caleb an American Embassy business card, the

American seal at the top, centered, majestic. On the card is her name and one phone number in big black letters. Noticing my inattentiveness, she says to Caleb, "If the police detain him, we have a United States marine on guard twenty-four hours a day. Call this number if he is held, locked up, or anything else like that and the marine will be there in minutes."

Caleb agrees, and just before we depart she warns us straight up: "Do not, under any circumstances, give the police any bribes. Do you understand?" She looks us both severely and squarely in the eye, devotes a full four seconds to each of us, "Sometimes bribing the police is not always in your best interest."

I am relieved. We have a get-out-of-jail-free card, and as we walk back to the city center on our way to the police station, Caleb and I hardly say a word to each other. I hear the city again, not the frantic voice inside my head detailing the different ways a big wooden stick can bash in my head. Instead, I hear the chickens *ca-rawing* at a miniature farm near the beach we pass. I see a beggar with no legs or arms swiveling on a sidewalk. I reach into my pockets to give him some money when I stop, and abruptly swing towards Caleb and say what's been on his mind since we left the embassy, he waiting for me to come to my senses, "What the hell are the police gonna do to me that would warrant that huge, corn-fed, M-16-haulin', camouflaged marine to come down and save me?"

Caleb chuckles his response: "I guess we're gonna find out."

The police station is a big ugly cement block, paint chipping off the exterior walls, not the same one that my previous muggers drove by when they threatened pain and death. Here, there is a dump right next door to the building and it smells foul with a couple of donkeys sniffing through the rubbish.

The walls of the police station are pink but dirty like some profoundly chemical sunset. The leaks in the ceiling erode the cement underneath the paint, flaking off sections from years of disrepair. Caleb and I stand at the counter for ten minutes, even wave at some of the twelve or thirteen police-men in the big room, but they are stubborn and pretend they have other things to do. They don't. They stare at us but don't approach or answer our entreaties. We sit on a pink chipped cement bench until finally a bony, tube-faced policeman comes to the counter and asks us to stand. I tell him the story about the stolen money in Zanzibar and the currency decla-ration form and the brothers Joseph and the Salamander restaurant on Samora Avenue and the delicious *chai*, and the taxi and the badges and the big wooden stick and the big marine and Barbara Johnson and I speak to the tube-faced man as fast as I can because I can see he isn't very interested and he cuts me off when I tell him about the betrayal of the brothers Joseph and tells me to sit down.

I sit down next to Caleb. We sit in silence while other cops watch us. The first policeman talks to a second policeman who comes to the counter and asks me to stand. He is not as lean as the first and has a tiny, bloody piece of chicken stuck between his two front teeth. I come to the counter and explain the story again. Meanwhile, Caleb goes to the other end of the counter and introduces himself to a couple of police who are talking and drinking coffee.

I tell my story again with the brothers Joseph and the Salamander restaurant and the big wooden stick and the money stolen and the currency declaration form and the fake badges and all of that. I tell my story to the policeman, the tiny piece of chicken taunting me each time the policeman yawns in my face. He hardly seems to be listening while Caleb laughs with the other policemen at the other end of the counter.

"You lie. Sit down," commands the piece-of-chicken-in-the-teeth policeman.

I am devastated and Caleb doesn't seem to notice. He is busy talking to one cop now while I ponder the rest of my days in a jail cell. I imagine the marine coming down like some camouflaged Rambo and shooting up the place to save me and I think of us scurrying out as he shoots his way out of the prison. Thirty minutes pass, Caleb still talking with five policemen now and I think about fleeing the country through some back road, through the Masai Mara, where I would have to evade elephants, hyenas, and spiny horned gazelles in order to avoid some bruised, bloody prison sentence.

A superior officer walks in from the back entrance into the dank room, carrying the stench of the garbage piles on the side of the building. He is fat by African standards and respected because all of the policemen salute with honest reverence as he walks in. I imagine for the second time today my crushed skull in my hands and I can't help thinking that Caleb lost the secret card with the American seal and the United States marine guard's private number, our personal bat phone. Can Caleb make a run for the American embassy before I am beaten to death? Will they let him in the embassy even though he is Australian? Will Caleb even bother?

The superior officer with gold-plated lapels walks over to Caleb, listens quietly while Caleb tells a joke to two other policemen, then saunters over to me. "Come here, tell me this story of yours."

He looks behind him in collusive mockery at the first

officer to whom I told the story. So I begin my story again, but this time, I say this, "For the past two hours I have told this story three times already and no one listens to me." He looks at me with no change in his face and waits. He has heavy jowls and his teeth are surprisingly straight.

I tell him about the boredom and the mistake I made initially by trusting the brothers Joseph. I tell him about the Salamander on Samora Avenue and the bouncy Coca-Cola legs and the currency declaration friend and the taxi my mother said I shouldn't get into and the big wooden stick and the pleading faces of the brothers Joseph and the speech about the Tanzanian economy and the threats and the prison and the big wooden stick and the little black boy chasing the chicken and the travelers' checks and the American embassy and the ever-trusting Barbara Johnson. I don't tell him about the big M–16-haulin' marine in camouflage. I decide that he is my ace in the hole.

He smiles a straight-toothed grin, unrelenting, and replies, "You are like all the rest. You come in here with these stories and you want us to write you a police report so that you won't get in trouble with immigration when you leave our country. You come in here and you tell your story and you think we will believe you. You exchange your money on the black market as if your American dollar couldn't already buy you everything already and you still come here, undermine our economy and you expect us to believe you, to help you. We are going to lock you up and take you to court because you are a criminal. That is how we do things here. Sit down!"

I almost cry because I have a sincere flashback to the knotty-faced man in the passenger side of the taxi waving that big stick in my face about to kill me. I sit down. Meanwhile Caleb talks with a growing number of police and he tells them another joke. They all laugh. Doesn't he see that I am about to be locked up, arrested, beaten, the key having already been lost and my fate having already been decided? Doesn't he see that my life is about to end here in the Dar es Salaam jail? Doesn't he see that?

Another hot, distressing ten minutes pass. Another officer comes in and commands me to the counter. He is shorter than the rest, pygmie size, and wears a red beret, carries a sidearm, and has red stripes on his left sleeve. He looks more like he's in the army than the police, though very much like a circus clown, too. I think he is higher in rank than the previous officer, or perhaps they sent him over to me because they like to watch me lose my brain slowly each time I tell the story. I am about to yell and scream and completely break down. My knees are weak and he asks me to tell the story again.

Again!

I inhale moist rank air, slouch, and tell him: The brothers Joseph, the boredom, the friend on Samora Avenue, the currency declaration *chai*, the maternally worried white woman traveler, the ID cards, the prison cab, the big wooden chicken, the black boy chasing the money, the speech, the three hundred dollars, the travelers' checks, the fake badges, the embassy, Barbara Johnson all dressed in camouflage. As I tell him this story, I can tell he doesn't care. He is already thinking about getting the keys to the prison cell in which they are going to lock me up, beat me, and leave me to die.

He interrupts the story, "Sit down. I am sorry, we must lock you up until we can verify your story." A tear develops in my left eye when Caleb and two other policemen approach, the policemen saluting the officer who has already left me to die in a prison cell. They talk in Swahili while Caleb tells me that he thinks everything will be all right.

I whisper emphatically to Caleb, "Bullshit! I am fucking good as dead. Get that fucking phone number and call that fucking marine and tell him that I am about to be locked up and beaten up and my bones will be broken and my blood will be let and I am going to my death! Call him, damn it. Call him before it is too late."

Though I think that the policemen can't hear me, they gawk at me obviously insulted, their necks craning forward in amazement when Caleb laughs out loud. I am going to punch Caleb in the stomach when he begins, "Do you remember that guy Mark Johnson we met at Ma Roaches guest house in Nairobi, that Australian guy who we had some beers with just before we left for Mount Kenya?"

"What the fuck are you talking about?!"

"Just listen, O.K.? Calm down and listen. Do you remember Mark Johnson?"

"Yeah…" I sigh. I notice four cops at the counter watching me go through this interrogation.

"And do you remember how he was planning to come to Tanzania for a few weeks before heading south to Zambia?"

"Yeah, I guess so…"

"And you remember how he was so friendly and seemed to know everyone in Nairobi?"

"Caleb. Enough. What is your fucking point?"

"Well this guy here, Samuel," he points to one of the policemen with whom he was talking for the past three hours, "he knows Mark Johnson, met him while Mark was passing through Dar. Samuel even showed me the address that Mark gave him, and I showed him the address that Mark gave us in Nairobi and it matches. It is the same address, the same Mark Johnson. It is the same guy!"

Before I punch Caleb in the stomach, or maybe I will

punch him in the face, Samuel, the policeman with whom Caleb was talking speaks up while the red-striped officer to whom I was speaking walks away.

"Any friend of Mark Johnson's is a friend of ours. What can we do for you? Do you need a police report, no problem."

I stare at Caleb, at the two friends he made and the policeman looks at me and says, "*hakuna matata, rafiki,*" which means, "no problem, friend." I am about to pass out and the tear in my left eye falls silently to the floor when Samuel, friend of Caleb, Samuel, friend of Mark Johnson, says to me, "I just need you to tell me exactly what happened."

For the fifteenth time I tell the story with the stolen money and Zanzibar and the boredom and the dust and the Josephs and the Salamander *chai* and the currency declaration bank and the last white woman I would ever see and the taxi that my mother said not to get into and the big wooden knot in the back of the guy's head and the black boy waving a big stick and the threats of death counting money and the stereo system warning me, comforting me, and the travelers' chickens and the whole thing and Barbara Johnson and the big wooden marine and all of that and when I stop, he says to me again, "*Hakuna matata rafikinini,*" meaning, "not to worry my friends." I am not worried anymore, but we are not out of this yet, and Caleb and I can feel it coming.

"I just need a hundred dollars, *rafiki,*" he continues, "before I can make out a false police report." A hundred dollars in Tanzania can support an extended family for a month but I am not about to get into any more trouble, fall into any more traps.

I mutter obscenities under my breath, dream of grabbing Samuel's throat and pummeling him, but regain my senses, bend my knees and steadily build my confidence.

"Listen. When I mentioned earlier the U.S. embassy consular official named Barbara Johnson, I meant to add that we have the direct phone number of the huge, Nebraskan, corn-fed, camouflaged M-16-haulin' marine, who guards the place. Would you like I should call him?"

I gestured to Caleb to show Samuel, friend of Caleb, friend of Mark Johnson, the American embassy card with the special embassy seal and the phone number in big black letters, "And the marine will come down here if you want or he can stay right where he is and Barbara Johnson won't need to know about any of this."

"O.K., O.K., friend, don't worry. O.K. Then we will make it fifty dollars. How about fifty." Samuel doesn't hesitate or change his mood. He is still very happy and I am pretty sure that we are going to get that report whether or not we pay him any money.

"Barbara Johnson also told me not to give you guys any money. Not a single cent. No bribes."

"O.K., O.K. *Hakuna matata*. Five dollars. That's all. Five dollars."

"NO!"

"O.K., O.K. You are a friend of Mark Johnson's. He is my friend too. Twenty shillings."

"I am sorry, friend. I cannot."

"O.K., O.K, don't worry friend, it's okay. *Hakuna matata*."

I sit down. Twenty minutes later the two friends of Mark Johnson tell us to come back at eight o'clock sharp the next morning to get the police report.

"Don't worry everything will be all right," Samuel says to me. I think of the Josephs, one on my right side telling me everything will be all right, one on my left side telling me to do as they say and I won't be hurt. We walk out to a hot greasy night. It is still Dar es Salaam and I am not dead.

✶

I sleep hard with intermittent fitful dreams. I dream of jumping over one of my brothers Joseph through the window and out of the moving taxi cab, only to be hit by a large beer truck making its daily run, driven by the chicken, of course. I dream of the small black boy waving a big wooden stick, chopping off my hands, then my arms, then my legs. I don't feel any pain, but I become a little stressed when my arms are gone. A loud thump chops off my left arm as a similar sound comes from the door to our room. I dream of my right arm falling to the ground with a loud thump when another bang on the door rattles our room. More thumps on the door, more limbs on the floor. I sit up, still dreaming, stressed about the mess my limbs are making on the floor of our room when I hear, "Open this door. I am the police!" A loud knock bangs again. My limbs disappear from the floor and I wake. Caleb wakes.

"What time is it?" I ask Caleb.

"It's six. Man, what the hell is going on here?"

We open the door and an elfin, wily, pitch-black African strides into the room and stands by our sink, looking our room over, looking at our beds, looking at our packs. He is so full of himself I almost laugh. His chest is puffed out and he is wearing huge mirrored sunglasses, the kind Starsky used to wear in *Starsky and Hutch*. But the more he talks, the more he reminds me of an African Foghorn Leghorn, the cartoon rooster. The beauty of it is he doesn't realize that he is a cartoon rooster and I am waiting for Rod Serling to pop out of the closet to tell us that we have all entered "The Twilight Zone."

"Can we help you?" I ask in utter disbelief. It is ridiculous that he thinks we would be awake, that it is customary for police to show up in travelers' rooms at six in the morning.

He doesn't answer at first and Caleb and I make a note to each other tacitly that we have reached the point of absurdity, of complete bizarreness.

"You can't go to the police station, there has been a problem with the police report. You can't go there or you might get in trouble."

He speaks English well but his tone is so serious that we are having a hard time taking him seriously. I feel like we are posing for a Salvador Dali painting. I look to see if this man has legs by checking the spaces between his shoes and his pants. There are black spaces there but perhaps he doesn't have socks and we are indeed about to enter into some fifth-dimensional universe.

Once my mind comes back to the Hotel Mbowe, I demand, "What are you talking about?" Cop or no cop, I am pissed. Six in the morning, what the hell is he doing here this early? I don't want to be in any weird painting and I don't need to be in any cartoon with a big puffed-up African rooster.

"There has been a problem with the police report. You can't go get it, I have to get it for you. You have to stay here and I will bring it to you."

"Why? We talked with Samuel last night and he said that we should be at the station at eight o'clock and everything would be fine. *Hakuna matata* and all that, *rafiki*, you know, *rafiki*?"

I wasn't about to give him any benefits of any doubts.

"All I know is if you go to the station, you will be put in jail, locked up, and I don't know what they will do to you. It is a set-up, you have to believe me." He slowly turned frantic, and threatening. And I, confused, still half asleep, wondering how this drama can get any worse, decide to take the hard tack. "Let me see your police badge."

He gives it to me. I open it up, it is different than the ones I saw when the bad guys abducted me. This one has his photo with the word P O L I C E in thick red ink across the top. I copy down his full name, his department, his badge number, all of it. Then I give it back to him.

His hands quiver slightly as he takes it. "Why did you do that? You didn't need to do that."

He is panicked. Caleb and I are delighted and shift into a more relaxed mood.

"Look sir," I say with a hint of mockery, because I can see fear develop through his mirrored sunglasses, "yesterday I was mugged, threatened, and almost beaten with a wooden stick. They used fake police identity cards and I need to know for sure you are really with the police; I don't know anything anymore and I am just being safe."

"You didn't need to do that. I am here to help you, not hurt you. You shouldn't have taken my name. I was going to get the report for you and bring it back here for you so there would be no trouble. Now I don't know what to tell you but you will definitely be in trouble now. When you get there, you just watch out. I will be there, and you will see, you will go directly to jail!"

The policeman abruptly leaves the room as suddenly as he had come in. Caleb and I let out a good laugh.

"What the hell was that all about?" I ask Caleb.

"That guy probably heard our story and wanted to bribe us. He would've brought the police report here and tried to sell it to us, that's all."

"I can't believe this. When will this all end?" I exclaim and go back to bed, though I don't sleep.

Eight o'clock comes around and we are at the police station and we ask for the police report which I can only assume will tell the whole story with the bus ride and the bumps and the boredom and the brothers Joseph and the man in the bank and the Salamander restaurant and the *chai* and the taxi cab and the big wooden stick and the threats of beatings and worse and the prison and the money stolen and the travelers' checks and the big corn-fed marine and all of it. Instead on a rough beige piece of paper, the police report simply reads in small blue ink-spotted letters:

CURRENCY DECLARATION FORM STOLEN

It is enough. And the puffed rooster of a Tanzanian who came to wake us up and extort money never appears. We don't look for him and besides, we are leaving tonight on the Tazara railway heading for Zambia. The border crossing we have heard is the most thorough one in all of East Africa. One traveler told us that you better have crossed all your T's and dotted all your I's because these guys check everything.

But I am not scared because I have already been through Hell in Dar es Salaam. I am not scared because I almost had my brains beaten into mush. I am not scared because I have seen the black boy chasing the chicken and they aren't portending my death anymore. I am not scared because my guardian angel while wheeling the deal to save my life also got me a three-month safe travel permit and it would be an insult to leave the African road after all he did for me. But most of all, I am not scared because I remember that Mark Johnson told us he was going to take the Tazara railway from Dar es Salaam to Lusaka, Zambia, and that is exactly where we are heading.

Jono Marcus has also traveled on frazzled shoestrings in Europe, Asia, Southeast Asia, and Baja California. He imports from Indonesia and is a grant-writing consultant in San Francisco.

* * *

The Monster Dildo

It just keeps popping up.

The thing was huge. When Paul pulled it out of the closet and waved it under my nose, I jumped back, jaw open, disbelieving. Dildos just aren't that BIG!

This mammoth, rubbery love stick had ended up hidden under piles of recycled paper and unclaimed sunglasses in an adventure outfitter's office in Northern California, but it originated in Mexico.

When I heard this true story, I just had to pass it on, a story that as yet has no end. The dildo keeps showing up at the most unexpected moments. It almost has a life of its own.

Paul leads commercial tours to Baja annually. Last winter, the group was heading back to the States and had stopped at a hot springs overnight somewhere near San Felipe. Wencil, one of the trip leaders, is a handyman kind of guy. After fielding a bunch of complaints that the toilet in the men's camp bathroom didn't work very well, he went to investigate.

Something was blocking the flow of water. When Wencil lifted the tank lid, he adjusted his eyes in the dim light and couldn't quite fathom what the object was that was stuffed into the tank. Pink, long, wide. A gargantuan dildo, just hanging out in the toilet bowl tank.

Wencil gingerly removed the obstruction with a towel. He sure as heck didn't want the others in his group to see him sporting this rubber wonder, so he wrapped it in the towel and made sure it didn't stick its head out. Not knowing what to do with it, and afraid he might embarrass the owner, he hid it under his sleeping bag and zipped the tent shut.

Sitting around the campfire that night, Wencil was having a hard time keeping this new-found thing a secret. He invited Paul to his tent when most of the others had gone to bed and presented this new member of their tour to Paul. After five minutes of disbelief and a running stream of "Oh my God, Oh my God, Oh my God," Paul, who is very social and loves to stir things up, took the torch, so to speak, and presented it to the people still gathered around the campfire.

After rolling around in the dirt for a while in hysterics, the group voted to place the almighty lingam on the breakfast table and deck it out altar-style for the breakfast crew. Flowers, candles, beads all adorned the now out-in-the-open phallic totem.

The next morning, the chef and her acolytes arose and found…the altar. For some reason they didn't think it was funny at all. Was it because they were all women? Or was it because they hadn't consumed coffee yet? A minor war of words occurred and Paul took the brunt of the blame, and faced-up to accusations of being an insensitive lout.

Paul decided to have a hanging, a purging. Lynch the plastic terror before anyone else felt traumatized by its gross size and innuendo of sadomasochistic sex. They wrapped a rope around its head and it swung from a tree for the rest of their stay in Agua Caliente.

When it was time to pack up and head north, the group couldn't just leave the thing there for other campers to ponder, so Paul cut it down and threw it in the woodbin on the side of the trailer.

Everyone forgot it until the roadblock. The Mexican police were pulling people over and inspecting vehicles. Things went fine as they walked around the van and trailer, which held Paul's tour group. Until one of the officers reached into the woodbin and pulled out the dick. He stood in glaring sunlight holding the sixteen-inch wand of love in his hand and asked "¿*Que es esto?*" or "What is this?" The other officers turned and looked at what he was questioning. They laughed uproariously for ten minutes, threw it back in the wood bin, and waved Paul and his tour forward. They didn't really want an answer!

The next morning, as the chef got out half-and-half for coffee, guess what was on ice? Mr. Pink himself. Someone in the group with a sense of humor had decided it was an organ transplant and needed to be preserved, especially since it had saved them at the road block, which many times requires a bit of bribing to pass through.

It resided in the ice chest next to the eggs and milk until the border. Because it was so popular with the last gang of Mexican police, Paul decided to show it to the customs officials. Well, his Spanish was at the halting, present-tense stage. He whipped it out of the ice chest and said, "This is a lethal weapon. Ha Ha?"

"Weapon?"—the officials asked suspiciously. A few hours later, after the ordeal of trying to explain to the police in broken Spanish, the dildo's history, Paul and friends were back on the road. This time the dildo got thrown in the trailer. People were getting tired of it. The novelty of a mascot dildo was wearing off. The group wanted to get home and get out of the van. They had been touring for two weeks.

Weeks went by. Business as usual. More trips for Paul and his adventure company. The new secretary didn't like the way the office was decorated, so she decided to rearrange things a little. Clean the place up, get rid of the piles of magazines and catalogs cluttering the floor. First she needed a place to put it all out of sight. The closet. She saw the dildo. It was back. No one knew how it got in the closet!

She was totally grossed out and tossed it, heaved it, over the fence. Only it didn't make it over the fence. It got stuck in a tree limb above the office entrance; a definite eye-catcher. It had to come down, but no matter how hard they shook the tree, it was lodged there. Finally they called Wencil. Wencil brought a construction ladder. The dildo went back in the closet.

It disappeared a month ago when Paul wanted to show me the star of this story. He was miffed, where did it go? Then last week, I asked about it again. Paul dug around in the closet. He gave a grunt of surprise on finding it back on the shelf beside the office supplies. He whipped it out. That was when I jumped back, mouth hanging open, totally intimidated by the size of the monster dildo from Mexico that just wouldn't go away.

Since the day she turned eighteen Lisa Alpine's restless spirit has lead her on journeys all over the globe. She is a professional writer and travel columnist and has woven her love of travel into her other passions—dance (www.danceweaver.com) and writing (www.lisaalpine.com). Lisa combines her interests in writing, storytelling, poetry, travel and dance into workshops around the world. She's also a proud member of the infamous Bay Area writing group, The Wild Writing Women.

* * *

Disbelief of Wonder

The African bush holds many mysteries.

"YOU WANT TO HEAR SOMETHING FUNNY?" THE YOUNG cook Cisco asked me in his native Botswanan accent, as he prepped a beef stew for dinner in our safari camp in Kasane, a town just outside the Chobe National Park in northern Botswana. "I hear there is a man from America who plays the piano, but he is blind." He chuckled as if it were some silly urban myth that all the kids in his hometown of Maun were told. Maun is a small town in the middle of the Kalahari Desert, so I guess it was more like a desert mirage.

"Oh, you mean Stevie Wonder?" I asked him.

"Yes, I think that is him," he answered. "He is a comedian?"

"No, he's a musician."

"And he is blind?"

"Yes," I told him. "You haven't heard of Stevie Wonder?" Evidently the world-famous Stevie Wonder wasn't known in the remote villages of Africa.

"If he is blind, then how can he see the keys of the piano?"

"I don't know. He just listens to the notes and feels his way around."

"Oh, so the music sounds bad and all mixed up?"

"No, he's really good. He plays a lot of songs. Haven't you heard of 'Ebony and Ivory'?" It would have been the perfect Ebony and Ivory moment between the two of us, talking together in perfect harmony, if not for my tan Filipino-American skin. It was more like Ebony and Coffee with Milk, Two Sugars.

"That is a song he plays?"

"He plays it and sings along."

"No, you are joking," he said, chuckling in doubt. His bright ivory smile glimmered between his dark ebony lips.

"No, he really does. He plays the piano and sways his head while he sings," I explained as I imitated Mr. Wonder's signature motions. "Sometimes he even plays the harmonica." My Stevie Wonder mimicking was more like the slithering of the indigenous spitting cobra and it made Cisco really start to laugh.

"You are a fool!" He tended to the campfire in disbelief.

"No, I'm not joking!"

He thought I was trying to pull a fast one on him, or just perpetuating the bucolic myth. So I had to do what America has done in the past: call in the British Army for backup — a fellow traveler in our safari group from London who had served in Her Majesty's armed forces.

"Bob, you know who Stevie Wonder is, right? Cisco here doesn't believe me that he's blind and can play the piano."

"Ah yes, Stevie Wonder," Private Bob said in his prim British accent. "He's a black American musician who is blind and plays the piano. He's quite famous really." The same information coming out of a respectable British soldier was enough to convince the skeptical Botswanan.

"I will have to tell my friends that it is true then. There *is* a man in America who is blind and can play the piano."

"Actually, there's another. Have you heard of Ray Charles?"

Cisco burst into laughter. "Ha ha! Oh, now I *know* you are just fooling me!" He shook his head and laughed and went away to make dinner. Oh, if only Stevie Wonder could see the smile on his face.

Erik R. Trinidad is a freelance travel writer and designer based in the metro New York City area. His exploits around the world have included wearing a tuxedo in Antarctica to try and blend in with the penguins, and wearing a bra during the Montreal comedy festival to try and blend in with the Canadians. Neither costume worked. Erik's collected stories can be read at www.TheGlobalTrip.com.

Cowboys and Indians, Thai Style

At Thailand's premier cowboy resort, a displaced traveler from Kansas explores the mysteries of the Far East's Wild West.

STANDING IN THE DUSTY STABLES OF PENSUK GREAT WESTERN cowboy resort, the wrangler sizes me up and tells me there's a problem. "You can't ride the horses," he says.

"Why not?" I ask.

"You're too fat."

I look down at my body, which is downright lanky. "Too fat?"

"Too fat!" The wrangler grins shyly and gives me a thumbs-up, as if this should be a compliment.

Perplexed, I set off to find Tammy, the Pensuk resort publicist, who's been acting as my informal ranch guide. I spot her near the front gate, where—dressed in Levis, leather chaps, and a Stetson—she is lighting incense at a small Buddhist shrine. "How much do you weigh?" she asks when I tell her what just happened.

"Maybe 180."

"Oh!" she says merrily. "You are too fat!"

"But I'm six-foot-three!"

Tammy gives me a sympathetic look. "This is an American-style cowboy ranch, but we don't get many Americans. The weight limit for our horses is 165 pounds. Maybe you would like a free beer instead? Or maybe more bullets?"

I ponder this for a moment. "I guess I'll take the bullets."

The Stetson-topped publicist reaches into her Levis and takes out a voucher for the rifle range. "Sorry about the horses," she says. "It's hard to find big ones in Thailand."

Taking the voucher, I count my losses and head off down the road in search of a little gunplay.

When I first heard that the plains of northeast Thailand were home to a popular cowboy resort catering to middle-class Thai vacationers, it sounded implausible to the point of being ridiculous. After all, millions of Western tourists flock to Thailand every year to enjoy world-class beaches, culture, and cuisine—and it would seem only natural that Thai tourists would also want to indulge in their own stretch of paradise.

But, as I have discovered this weekend, scores of Thai holidaymakers would much rather play cowboys and Indians at this sprawling Western theme-ranch, located some two hundred miles northeast of Bangkok. According to Tammy (whose Thai name is Thanawan Chanlar), Pensuk's sixty log cabin and teepee-style rooms are booked up months in advance, year-round. "Thai people love Thailand, but they also want to try something different," she told me. "They think that cowboy life is very exciting."

Since I grew up in Kansas, the idea of Thais shunning the wonders of Thailand for an artificial vision of the American West carries a weird kind of echo. When I was a kid, the only tourist attraction within three counties of my home was Wichita's "Cowtown"—an open-air "living history museum" along the banks of the Arkansas River. There, men dressed as cowboys performed lasso tricks, gave lectures about Wichita's cattle-drive heyday, and occasionally re-enacted gunfights. Cowtown was interesting enough, but after my third or fourth school field trip, the place had lost its appeal. I began to dream about other places, far from the doldrums of the plains—places with turquoise waters, white-sand beaches, and jungle-covered mountains. Places, in short, like Thailand.

Hence, it feels a tad strange to be walking through a stretch of Thailand that bears an uncanny resemblance to Cowtown. Horses trot along the main road as I make my way toward the rifle range; a cluster of teepees sits by the roadside; cornfields stretch into the distance. A frontier-town strip called "High Hill"—which features saloons, barbershops, and a Chinese laundry—anchors the center of the resort.

Despite such nods to authenticity, however, it's quickly obvious that this ranch is operated and patronized entirely by Asians. In the saloon, for instance, draft beer is served with ice cubes, and the menu features *paad thai* and fried rice. Inside the various buildings, the cowboy décor is a befuddled jumble of spaghetti western, long-haul trucker, and American pop-culture motifs. Air-brushed murals of coyotes, cacti, and voluptuous Indian women line the walls of the teepees. An American flag hanging in one of the cabins has the image of an eighteen-wheeler painted across its stripes. The main road through the resort is marked with "Route 66" signs, and the decidedly anomalous karaoke lounge features oversized pictures of Elvis Presley and Marilyn Monroe.

All of this is in addition to the ubiquitous outdoor loudspeakers, which broadcast pop-country hits to all corners of the ranch: As I make my way toward the rifle range, I find myself humming along to "I Never Promised You a Rose Garden."

When I arrive, I find a seat in the waiting area next to a youngish Thai man named Phon.

"But you can call me Diamond," he tells me.

"What, like Diamond Jim rodeo hats?" I ask.

"Like Neil Diamond, the cowboy singer."

"Oh, of course. Having a good time here?"

Diamond smiles and thumbs the brim of his hat. "I love it here," he says. "It makes me feel like I'm Clint Eastwood. When I was young, I wanted to go to America so I could enjoy this kind of freedom, but now I can do it right here in Thailand."

"What kind of freedom do you mean?"

"Oh, you know. American freedom: Riding horses and shooting guns. It's a great way to spend my holiday."

"But what about the natural parts of Thailand? Don't you like beaches or the mountains?"

"Thailand is nice, but the beaches are full of fishermen, and the mountains are full of hill tribes. Those are country people; they aren't very sophisticated. It's more interesting to come here. It's more civilized—just like your country."

Five minutes later, Diamond takes his turn at the rifle range, where he happily blasts away at the paper targets. As I watch him, I feel a little unsettled by his narrow, romanticized vision of America. Like the other Thais I've seen at Pensuk, Diamond's passion for range life appears to be inseparable from his love of cowboy movies. Imagine a Texas-based Asia theme park that interprets the Orient through kung-fu films, and you get a basic idea of how the Thais here interpret the American West.

This said, I'd reckon it goes both ways: were Diamond to

hang out with American tourists on their superficial forays into Theravada Buddhist meditation retreats or Patpong go-go bars, he would no doubt be similarly annoyed. Like tourism anywhere, fascination with other cultures is as much a matter of image and fantasy as it is tradition or reality. Just as Americans are drawn to Asian culture by fictional sources such as *Crouching Tiger, Hidden Dragon*, many Asians prefer to see America through the lens of *The Good, the Bad, and the Ugly*. Pensuk resort simply saves Thais the trouble of traveling around the world only to be disillusioned.

After shooting my own share of bullets, I return to my air-conditioned teepee to prepare for Pensuk's marquee event—a cowboy-and-Indian dinner-show extravaganza listed in my brochure as "Drunk Man Cowboy and His Gang—Stunt + Effect." The event takes place in an outdoor plaza just beyond the storefronts of High Hill town, and Tammy seats me at a table up near the stage. At the edge of the plaza, imitation chuck wagons dispense a variety of spicy Thai dishes (Tex-Mex food, Tammy notes, has yet to catch on). Onstage, a Thai heavy metal band in checkered shirts and straw cowboy hats plays note-perfect covers of Hank Williams and Garth Brooks tunes. Occasionally the band sneaks in a number by Pink Floyd or Black Sabbath, but the one hundred or so Thais in attendance don't seem to mind as they queue around the chuck wagons. Once everyone has had a go at the buffet line, the cowboy-and-Indian show commences.

Though I don't know enough Thai to catch all the nuances of "Drunk Man Cowboy and His Gang," I'm soon convinced that I've stumbled upon the single most politically incorrect depiction of Western life ever performed in public. Indeed, after less than a minute of narrative back-story, the whole production erupts into a paroxysm of violence: Thai cowboys in Lone Ranger masks rush out to slap squaws, lasso braves, chug beers, and shoot off their six-guns; grease-painted Indians whoop, slash scalps, guzzle whiskey, and brandish spears. Fists fly, tables are overturned, and (in what I presume is the "stunt" portion of the show) several combatants are hurled bodily into buildings and fence posts. In one corner of the stage, a musician from the heavy metal band simulates all the punching noises on an electronic keyboard.

After a prolonged melee, a young Indian is dragged up onstage, stripped to his buckskin trousers, and mock-beaten by the cowboys for ten solid minutes. Then—just when I'm certain that the John Wayne violence is going to degenerate into something more suited to John Wayne Gacy—the stage lights go down, Billy Ray Cyrus's "Achy Breaky Heart" booms out from the sound system, and a trio of Thai cowgirls starts line-dancing on the roof of a High Hill town storefront. When this finishes, a paunchy Thai Indian chief strolls out into the audience, tells a few jokes (complete with vaudeville snare-rolls from the heavy metal drummer), and launches into a spirited rendition of Elton John's "Crocodile Rock." As the final notes of the song fade out, the stage lights flash back on, and the cowboys resume beating the bejesus out of the half-naked Indian boy.

Although these abrupt transitions are accompanied by bits of Thai-language narration, I am nonetheless struck by the surreal grandeur of it all. Indeed, if "Drunk Man Cowboy and His Gang" ever gets produced for video, I suspect it would find a huge cult following among teenage stoners.

Of course, the video version would miss out on the interactive element—which becomes apparent when the cowboys drag the hapless Indian boy into the dining area and invite audience members to take turns slugging him. To my amazement, table after table of blushing salarymen and giggling housewives stand up to get their simulated licks in. Cameras flash and spectators applaud as devastating gut-shots and bone-crunching uppercuts are administered to the crisp accompaniment of the heavy metal keyboard.

While this spectacle snakes its way through the dining area, Tammy leans over and gives me a rather apologetic explanation. "If you make the cowboy show too polite, the customers don't like it," she says. "We tried to make it more historical, but the customers got bored. So now the show is mostly just fighting."

Eventually, the brawl makes its way back up onto the stage, where the evening's entertainment ends with a surprise Indian triumph. The audience is handed flaming bamboo torches and invited to join the Indians in whooping around a bonfire, and—not wanting to be a killjoy—I join in on the action.

As I take a torch and chant along with the victory song, it's easy to see how some people might see this part of Thailand as a distinctly negative symptom of cultural globalization. But from what I've experienced, this spectacle belongs to the realm of human nature as much as anything. Just as the Californians who seek temporary solace in Nepali ashrams are indulging in an essentially American ritual, Pensuk's cowboy reverie is an honest expression of the Thai people who seek it out—a celebration not of place, but of mood, novelty, and momentary escape from the banal parameters of reality. For all the talk of authenticity, cross-cultural travel invariably comes down to this: a rather limited indulgence in whatever we find most appealing about other parts of the world.

Out in front of the stage, I whoop along with the Indians.

I dance in circles and wave my torch. I look up at the stars, and dream that I'm sitting on a faraway stretch of Thai coast-line, sipping a beer and digging my toes into the brilliant white sand.

Rolf Potts's karaoke rendition of "Thank God I'm a Country Boy" has astonished and horrified audiences on four continents. He is the author of Vagabonding: An Uncommon Guide to the Art of Long-Term World Travel, *and his travel stories have appeared in* Salon.com, Condé Nast Traveler, National Geographic Traveler, National Geographic Adventure, Best American Travel Writing 2000, *and several Travelers' Tales anthologies. He keeps no permanent address, but his virtual home can be found at www.rolfpotts.com.*

More Ketchup than Salsa

A kiss is just a kiss—well, maybe.

A NUN WITH A BLACK MOUSTACHE HELD IN HIS STOMACH AND lifted his arms to allow me to pass. From one hand, Marlboro ash drifted down like confetti, and from the other, the contents of a plastic glass rained onto the hood of his devotional partner, bringing forth a burst of slurred Spanish that I suspected contained few sacred references.

The crowd around the refreshment kiosk was four deep, and from behind a pungent leg of cured ham I tried in vain to get the attention of the sunken-eyed barmen, their white shirts completely drenched from serving endless *cubatas* (Pampero rum and coke) and *churros* (deep fried doughnuts) in the heavy heat of the Canarian night.

Taped music from more than a hundred outdoor bars competed against the many bands dotted around the Plaza de España and adjoining Plaza de la Candelaria. The ensuing cacophony provided a head-spinning riot of salsa rhythms that were hard to follow even for the more experienced dancers.

The small pockets of non-Hispanic tourists who had traveled to Tenerife from all over the globe to participate in this, the third largest Carnival in the world, were clearly conspicuous amongst the throes of lithe, hip-swaying locals. Unable to synchronize their bodies with the unfamiliar Latin metre, they found themselves awkwardly trapped between the mechanical movements of a school barn dance and jiggling up and down in the manner of a desperate person finding himself at the wrong end of a distressingly lengthy toilet queue, resulting in more ketchup than salsa.

I had left my girlfriend Joy near the row of delightfully named *pipís moviles* (mobile toilets), and returned with drinks in hand just in time to see her being whisked into the mêlée by an old man who bore an uncanny resemblance to the late Walter Matthau. She waved a not altogether happy greeting as her surprisingly athletic companion tossed her from side to side. I raised a glass to toast her new-found friendship and the toast was returned with the mouthing of a word pertaining to having no father.

It was also returned by the most exquisite female form that I have ever had the boldness to raise a glass to, purposefully or inadvertently. She was some three feet beyond Joy and Walter, her tall slender body provocatively curved and arched under the spell of Latin fever. I realized that I may have been standing with my mouth ajar for several minutes and snapped it shut, swallowing hard as the girl shimmered and shimmied towards me.

"¿*Quieres bailar?*"

I nodded that I would indeed like to dance and set the two glasses down.

After many hazy minutes of inhaling pheromone-flooded perfume and being face to face with a perfect blend of doe-eyed innocence and deep-tanned allure while performing intimate gyrations that, but for the absence of a fleecy bed sheet and the presence of a hundred thousand onlookers, could have plausibly been called sex, I realized that Joy must have been tiring of the windscreen-wiper choreography of Mr. Matthau and was probably in some danger of suffering from whiplash.

I motioned apologetically to my dance companion that I had to leave and went to rescue Joy but not before the girl clasped the back of my head, pressed soft lips onto mine and thrust a probing tongue into my lungs. Startled, to say the least, I backed away, grabbing her hands and lowered them to a safer level. It was at this point that words, "What the hell…" hastily traveled from brain to mouth.

A carpet of hair covered the back of her, or as I now realized, *his*, hands. The salsa became slurry; a hundred thousand people turned to stare and visions of hairy legs of cured ham filled my mind. Quickly I sidled off into the masses and without a word grabbed Joy by the wrist and shouldered my way through the crowd to the nearest provider of steadying *cubatas*.

I'd been burned by a hot salsa. It was still a damn fine kiss though!

Joe Cawley is a freelance travel writer who contributes to the Sunday Times. *Based in the Canary Islands, he is medically forced to travel to relieve sporadic bouts of island fever that urge him to scream obscenities at the top of his lungs and which brings out an uncontrollable rash.*

* * *

Bushwalk

Don't try this one at the office.

THERE THEY STOOD, RIFLES IN HAND, A BLACK LAD AND A white lad in shorts with thighs hardly larger than his calves (a commentary on his thighs, not his calves). The first thing they did was to send me back to change my shirt; I happened to have on a red one, which was too noticeable, they told me with knowing looks. I returned in blue, and one of the men explained that the rifles were to protect us in case of need. We were to walk single file and not talk while walking. If we wanted their attention we should give a little whistle or softly click our fingers. It all sounded very thrilling! I saw myself softly clicking my fingers as I saw a pride of lions bearing down on us at full throttle.

Off set our little party of six, led by the two guides. For three hours we would be behind the electrified fence, where all the wild things are! The guides were also in single file, the one in front looking straight ahead, the second one looking alternately left and right. Everything was covered except our asses. We walked across a riverbed and the guides stopped, one of them pointing out the spoor (or "footprint" for those not in the know) of a black rhino. It looked about the size of a baseball glove. We looked around, half expecting to see this titanic creature thundering towards us, about to skewer all eight of us on his horn, like so much shish kabob. No such luck; there was no rhino to be seen, only this transient impression of his presence.

On we went through the bush, the guides stopping from time to time, explaining things biological. Of particular interest was dung. Dung told a lot. Dung sung, as it were, like a canary, telling what kind of animal had dropped it and whether it had been deposited there recently or some time ago. (As one would expect, "steaming" indicated very recent passage, and degrees of dryness indicated times past.) The passage of dung and urine is a way of sending a signal: this is my territory, friend, so keep out—or at least be nice and subservient! Scrape marks in a pile of the stuff indicated where a dominant bull rhino had scraped his hooves in it so that he would leave a scent trail demarcating his turf. Other males are allowed to drop a load, but they're not allowed the privilege of scraping their feet in it. (I realized from this explanation that dogs, when they kick feebly at their shit, are not trying to clean up after themselves with flabbergasting devolutionary inadequacy, but are actually trying to spread it about so as to tell other dogs who's the boss.)

Strange, I thought, that this message-sending function of dung does not appear in humans. Humans are generally uneasy about their evacuations—particularly their defecations—and are embarrassed and even ashamed of them, going so far in "hygienic" societies as to try and disguise the scent with perfumed sprays. When and why did this reversal of the patterns of behavior of our "lower" relatives occur? Imagine life if it

hadn't happened, with bosses not only figuratively but literally spreading their shit around in public, while their under-
lings were compelled to make small, subservient piles of it,
indicative of their rank.

I continued my musings as we hiked, and imagined the
boardroom: the boss comes in and greets the lesser mortals
seated around the table; he lowers his trousers, and, after some
trouble, manages to deposit a huge, steaming pile. He had to
perform because his position depends upon it; he scrapes his
wingtips in the revolting mess and drags them around the
table; all the middle-managers bend over and sniff, getting the
message; then they all lower their trousers and strain to produce modest piles, one slightly larger than the next; the boss
examines their constipated ordure and is satisfied; they all
clean up as best they can (but it's a messy job) and, after having nosed their way through the hierarchy, they put their
noses into their work. One could imagine many such scenar-
ios, from the lecture hall to the doctor's surgery.

True, the dung of herbivores is pretty mild stuff, with
nothing like the stench of that of the carnivores—although
the hyena's (surprisingly, considering this animal's image and
reputation) is also rather pleasant, being white and powdery
from all the calcium-rich bones it devours.

On and on we walked, avoiding as best we could the aca-
cia's spikes. At the end of the walk we had seen many insects
but only one animal: an obliging little bush bok, who probably felt sorry for us. But, my goodness, we had seen a terrific
amount of dung! This is what we leave behind, and even this
is short-lived, soon to be absorbed in the great cycle of life,
only to be shat out again.

*Eugene Sigaloff is a writer living in The Netherlands. This story is an
excerpt from a journal he kept while traveling through Mozambique.*

Crossing Borders

*Between Canada and the U.S.—even
before 9/11—lay a Twilight Zone.*

I JUST LEFT MY LIFE BEHIND AND AM HEADING TO THE OTHER
side of it. The other side of it is called California, the land of
iced organic nonfat decaf soy mochas at every small town
street corner, t-shirts any day of the year, taco stands in the
desert, orange trees on front lawns and avocado trees in the
back; the land of redwoods and palms and palm readings
down the road, mountains almost everywhere and a 1,200-
mile view of the sea. It's the land of Tom Waits drinking tea
in a backwoods café. I saw him once. He ordered the tea with
his gravelly voice and when he got up to leave, he turned
around to smile at me as if we were in one of his songs.

California, I've wanted you all my life. You're almost on the
horizon, although I can still see my hometown of Guelph,
Ontario, Canada in the rearview mirror and California is
2,500 miles west of here.

I'm driving a blue beat-up Ford Bronco that I've decided
to call Marcia, in honor of Marcia Clark, the prosecuting at-
torney in the O.J. Simpson trial. I didn't want the Bronco to

remind me of O.J. Simpson who tried to escape down the LA freeway in a Ford Bronco with a disguise, ten thousand dollars, and a pistol to his head. Next to me sits a woman I've decided to call Morticia, although I call her that only in my mind. She's wearing a black polyester dress draping down to her ankles on one of the hottest days of the year and her long hair is dyed the color of slick tar. Enough black makeup is painted around her eyes to frighten small children and her face is unnaturally pale. Her real name is Debbie. I've just learned Morticia is twenty-eight, which seems a little old to be decked out in this sort of Goth get-up, or whatever they call it, especially when we're about to cross the border from Canada into the U.S. and I can't imagine the American border patrol will take kindly to her freakish attire.

Morticia is with me because she read the notice I placed on the University of Guelph ride board: CALIFORNIA OR BUST. LEAVING NEXT WEEK. CALL IF YOU WANT TO COME ALONG AND SHARE DRIVING AND GAS.

Debbie was the first reasonable person to call, or so she sounded on the phone. Before that, I'd had a variety of calls, all sounding like potential nut cases, although the seventeen-year-old named Jason who wanted to move to the desert and start his own band could have been inspiring. The middle-aged Polish woman who was escaping her "very mean and very ugly" husband could have been trouble, and the student who said he'd never consider sleeping anywhere but in a hotel was a definite no. Hadn't he ever slept in his car even once? Thrown his sleeping bag on the ground in a field under the stars one night? What was wrong with twenty-two-year-olds these days?

I liked Debbie right away. She sounded fun. Debbie said she was a grad student and she wanted a ride to St. Louis,

Missouri, where her boyfriend lived. St. Louis is only twelve hours from Guelph, not even a third of the way to California, but she sounded so high-spirited and level-headed on the phone, I said yes. We spoke over the phone again a few times to make arrangements but we didn't meet in person until today when I picked her up at her place in one of the student housing areas of town, a neighborhood of tall trees, large old houses in varying stages of disrepair, and dented cars parked on the road with bumper stickers saying things like *Think Globally, Act Locally* and *Mean People Suck* and *Think Whirled Peas!* The woman who answered the door seemed to be dressed for Halloween even though this is June.

"Is Debbie here?" I asked. "We're driving to St. Louis."

"That's me. I'm almost done packing. Hold on. Oh, nice to meet you."

I waited on her front porch under the scorching sun while she disappeared into the darkness of the house. I heard laughter inside but couldn't see any faces through the screen door. From somewhere in the back of the house a male voice said, "Are you really taking that thing, Deb? Hot damn!" When she reappeared on the porch carrying a knapsack, a black leather case, and a rolled-up army sleeping bag I couldn't help noticing she was beautiful. She thrust her hand out to shake mine, the old-fashioned gesture of it taking me by surprise. Under the layers of black fabric she seemed to carry herself with the grace of someone with long, slender limbs and a slow gait. Her eyes, beneath the metallic layers of eye shadow, were large and green and of an uncommon clarity, almost childlike, as if they were focused at a wider angle than most, allowing more of the world inside. Although her straight hair was dyed black from her ears down, its roots were shades of mahogany and red-like tones of wood polish. Her skin looked as if it had never been touched by the sun, the color of cream, and although some sun would have given it a cherry glow, she hadn't a single line or wrinkle.

As we walked toward my car she struggled with the zipper of her leather case which wouldn't close because the case was bulging full of clothes. When I helped her hold the case while she pulled the zipper I noticed that on top of some folded black jeans, a long strip of leather was coiled around itself like a black snake. "Looks like a belt, doesn't it?" she said.

"I guess. Is it?"

"It's a whip!" she said as she yanked the zipper across the top. She tossed the case and sleeping bag into the back of my car, hopped in the front seat, waved out the window and shouted goodbye at the house. As we drove off, she chuckled to herself, as if she knew something I didn't. *Terrific*, I thought. *I'll tell the American border guards she's my cousin and I'll be dropping her off at the Beat Me in St. Louis S&M convention,* LEATHER AND CHAINS R US. *I should have gone for the Polish woman with the mean husband after all.*

Morticia and I have been trying to have a conversation but I think her outfit is getting in the way. It's as if we're from different countries and we don't know the right questions to ask. Already I can tell we're both the sort who prefer asking questions rather than answering them, at least in the beginning. This conversation is like a game we're playing, tossing a hot potato back and forth as fast as we can so we don't have to think things through, so it doesn't burn us.

"So how long are you going to be in St. Louis?" I lean toward the open window to let the wind cool my face.

"Don't know yet. I have to wait and see how I like it. Why are you going to California?" Her feet on the dash. She's wearing army boots. The heat, I keep thinking. I'm in sandals and even they seem too hot today.

"I love California. I've been there lots of times. Hot day for a drive. Too bad I don't have air conditioning. So you're visiting your boyfriend in St. Louis?"

"Yep. Can't wait. What's so great about California?"

I turn to look at her eyes again, but this time I don't notice their clarity, but how they're expertly rimmed with smooth black eyeliner that grows gradually thicker from the inside until it reaches the iris and then tapers dramatically to a feathery tail just beyond the corner of her eye. I'm wearing cut-off shorts, a cotton sleeveless top, and no makeup. Suddenly I feel very unfashionable. "Lots of things. The coast for one thing. Most of the California coast is rugged and undeveloped. People don't realize that. They associate California with L.A. But so much of the state is wilderness. It's full of scenic beauty. So what are you studying?"

"Physics. And some other stuff. What are the people like there?"

"Physics?" I look over to see she hasn't rolled down her window at all. I find this incredible.

"I'll probably keep studying but not physics. The Californians. What are they like?"

"I guess you find all types there. The place is full of variety. People actually from the state and all kinds of people who've left winter and pollution and their old lives somewhere else." I put my left foot up on the dash. It feels good on a hot day. "California's very progressive, lots of environmentalists, social activists. No smoking allowed in public in the whole state, not in bars, restaurants. They don't even allow it in outdoor cafés out there. But it doesn't seem to matter much because hardly anyone seems to smoke there anymore.

They talk about it as if it's kind of a quaint and embarrassing idea from the past." I pass a slow-moving RV. "Where are you from?"

"Toronto originally." She picks up her knapsack and begins rifling through it. "You?"

"Guelph. I was born in the States but grew up in Guelph mostly." She's looking intently for something. Cigarettes perhaps.

"I have way too much stuff in this thing. So how long are you going to California for?" She's emptying the knapsack's contents onto her lap. One by one the items tumble out—a giant hairbrush, a clear plastic make-up bag, two tattered paperbacks, comic books that appear to feature leather-clad women in black masks holding whips, an electric toothbrush…

"For the summer," I tell her, although it could be much longer. I might actually be moving there for good. "Hey, comics. I used to love *Archie* comics. Betty and Veronica were my favorites."

"No way. Me too." For a second her eyes flash wide. "They're worth a lot, if you have the right ones and they're in good shape."

"There must be five hundred *Archies* in my parents' crawl space," I tell her. Maple forests stretch back from both sides of the highway, occasionally interrupted by a dairy or cattle farm. I look at the collection of odds and ends piled on the black clingy nylon of Morticia's lap. She must be boiling in those clothes but she's not even sweating. She actually seems cool. I keep thinking she'll explain something about herself, like her appearance, but after over an hour's drive it doesn't seem she will. Couldn't she have ditched the costume just for today? For months there have been articles in the papers about the American border guards cracking down ferociously on anyone entering the States. They're being nasty to anyone, Canadians included. But they don't want to discriminate, which seems vaguely at cross purposes. Just last week there was a piece in the news about them turning back two middle-aged Canadian women who wanted to go to New York state for the day to visit one of their daughters. Turned them back as if they were drug dealers.

"Is that rain?" she asks. Big drops are starting to spatter the windshield. The sky has become suddenly leaden.

"Yeah, rain will be nice. Cool things down. I love summer rains."

"Me too," she says. "I love how rain smells." She takes a deep breath and closes her eyes. We're discussing the weather. She's dressed as a witch for Christ's sake. Is this supposed to pass without comment? "Smells like dust rising," she adds.

Like dust rising? I'd expect someone so urban-looking, dressed as if she prefers the night and all its dark offerings, midnight taxi rides and full moon coven get-togethers for instance, wouldn't care or even know about the smell of summer rain showers. Yet she does. She tells me how as a kid she'd run into the street during thunderstorms, how her mother hated it, how she loved to feel drenched. Our conversation turns to Lewis Carroll, whom she loves. The rain is pounding harder, instantly cooling the air like a gift. Cars have switched on their headlights and I can hardly see the highway. Morticia and I discuss European medieval history and poetry. She likes T.S. Eliot and Emily Dickinson. Me, too. This is wonderful. Morticia is thoughtful and self-possessed, a bright mind with a youthful confidence, happy even. Why does she need to show the world this dark image of herself? Is it a reflection of a personal tragedy she's projecting?

Perhaps it's more subtle, something fragile and vulnerable deep within her that's not apparent by anything other than the way she presents herself, this physical fact of her black outfit. Possibly she's rejecting society at large in order to woo something else, something unknown to others, some primitive fear, something mystical and revered. Maybe it's fashion, something she and her friends can wear to be distinguished in a crowd, to pretend they're different, more interesting than the rest of us, possessors of a secret knowledge. Maybe she thinks black is her color. I can't fathom what it could be but perhaps that's what separates the young from the rest of us. The young, meaning anyone under thirty, are still open to the world, still believe it can be new, offer fresh ideas. Many of us over thirty have started shutting the door on anything new. We've grown suspicious, weary. We've already allowed enough of the world in to last us a lifetime. Anything new would be confusing.

"So are you excited about seeing your boyfriend?"

"God yes." She peers in her knapsack again and looks up, puzzled, as if she can't remember if she brought something.

"So how long have you known him?" The rain is splashing the side of my face and feels so good I leave the window open.

"Over a year now."

"How did you meet him?"

"On the net. There it is! It was in the pocket!" She holds out a Kit Kat chocolate bar in front of her with both hands.

"I didn't know they still made Kit Kats. No kidding, the net? On a chat line or something?" I glance over to see she's still holding the chocolate bar up to the windshield like a trophy. Somehow this lightens my heart. "Remember Bar Six? You can't get Bar Sixes anymore. Or Pixie Stix either. So, a chat line?"

"We like the same music, Alex and I, that's his name. Kind of a music chat line."

"Really? What's he like?"

"He's funny. Super intelligent, a little out there. Lives in his head, one of those types. Pretty cute too, sounds like." She offers me two 'sticks of the Kit Kat, half of it.

"Thanks. Sounds like? Sounds like what?" I bite into the melted chocolate.

She takes a bite and chews slowly, contemplating; then, scrunching up the red wrapper she says suddenly, "Like he's cute, not that he's actually said that about himself, but I can tell a lot about him by the way he writes. I know more about him than I do about my own brother. It's amazing what you can learn about a person you've never seen."

"You've never seen him?" I keep my eyes on the road but say it cheerily, so she'll go on.

"No. That's why I'm going to St. Louis, to see him."

"Oh… right." I swallow the last of my Kit Kat. The rain has stopped as suddenly as it arrived and already the sky is brightening. A sign saying "Bridge to the United States" is ahead. We pay a toll fee and cross the half-mile expanse over the St. Clair River where it flows out of Lake Huron. The view from the bridge is a glorious surprise. The sun has escaped from the rapidly moving clouds and its reflection on the water is blinding. A rainbow enlivens the sky and far below sailboats emerge looking like toys. At the end of the bridge we drive straight up to the immigration booth without having to wait in a line. I say hello and smile at the white-haired man behind the glass. He slides open his little window.

"Nationality?"

"Canadians."

"Purpose of visit?"

"Vacation."

"Where are you going?"

"I'm going to California and she's going to St. Louis."

The man leans out the window to get a closer look. Morticia twists her wrist up to give him a wave. He takes a deep uncompassionate breath. "Yeah, right, and I was born yesterday."

"Excuse me?"

"Would you mind telling me where you're really going?"

I repeat what I just told him.

"Look ladies. I don't have time for this. Where are you going today?"

"Why wouldn't we be going to California and St. Louis, Missouri?" Don't people go to those states? We have to go somewhere. I look over at Morticia. She shrugs. Maybe he thinks someone who looks like Morticia wouldn't be caught dead in the Bible-belted flatness of the Midwest. I turn back to the border guard. "Would it make a difference if I said Chicago? Nevada?…South Dakota?"

Instead of listening to me he writes something on a little piece of paper. "Pull your vehicle over there and step inside the main building." The man hands me the piece of paper and with no warmth in his voice whatsoever says, "Think about telling the truth once you're inside."

We pull into the mostly empty parking lot and stop the car. Morticia says to me quickly, almost under her breath, "Let's just say we're both going to California."

"But why?" I ask, incredulous.

"Because it sounds weird to say we're going to two different places."

"Why? We have nothing to hide. We just tell them the

truth. If we lie they'll trip us up. There's no point. Let's just tell them the exact truth. We're not doing anything illegal."

"But they don't trust the Internet. Don't tell them I met Alex on the Internet."

"O.K. I doubt they'll ask that anyway. This should be over in five minutes." As I open the car door I glance into the back seat at my pile of things. It's true. I have nothing to hide. When they search the car they'll see my tent, my camping gear, my books, my maps of the Rockies, maps of California, my hiking guides, Morticia's whip. What's the big deal? I begin to feel my pumping heart as we walk to the inspection station.

The spacious, air-conditioned U.S. Immigration building, impeccably clean with freshly painted white walls, is a far cry from the bleak and gray immigration offices I've seen in the Third World. Those offices usually have peeling paint, cheap fluorescent lights, too few windows, and men standing around holding unreasonably large guns. Sometimes, giant warning signs declare, "Anyone Caught With Drugs Will Be Hung." Things never seem on the up and up in those Third World immigration offices.

Another white-haired man is waiting for us, although this one's hair shoots up in mean military spikes like a bristle brush, perfectly flat on top. Steel blue eyes narrow to slits as he watches us take the long walk up to his counter. He taps his fingers on the surface. Four or five people behind him sit at computer screens in a brightly-lit office. When we arrive at the counter he doesn't say anything at first but continues tapping his fingers, eyeing us, and then, "Your story?"

"For some reason the guy out there didn't believe us." I hand him the piece of paper that seems to be written in scrawl, perhaps in code. "I'm going to California and I'm dropping her off in St. Louis."

"Aha," he says, "and why should he believe you?" He's still tapping his fingers.

"Because it's the truth. Don't people go to California anymore? Do you want to see my maps of California? Addresses of friends I have there? What can I show you?"

"Some identification for starters." His tongue is perched on the side of his mouth as if that's its usual resting place. He has a crowded bulldog face.

I fish through my bag and produce a driver's license, a library card, and some other photo I.D. Canadians and Americans aren't usually required to show a passport when crossing each other's borders so I never take mine with me when entering the States.

"What do you do for a living?"

"I'm a teacher." I don't tell him I'm also a writer. That sounds suspicious to people like him.

"Teacher?" He turns around to the people behind him at the computer screens and shouts, "She's trying to tell me she's a teacher!" A few of them look up from their screens, not particularly interested.

"Why wouldn't I be a teacher?"

"You don't look like a teacher to me." Again, that narrowing of his eyes set back in his hardened face.

"Why not?" Does he think all teachers wear hair spray, navy suits, and sensibly flat shoes?

"So if you're a teacher you're really smart. You should know all the capital cities."

"I know capital cities. Try me."

His eyes are mere slits now. For some reason he doesn't want to play this geography game after all.

"What do you teach?" He turns around. "Listen to this, guys." The office people don't seem to be listening.

"Lots of different things. High school English, E.S.L., adult education. I used to teach...."

"Prove you're a teacher."

In my wallet I find my teacher identification card, something I acquired ages ago, after teacher's college, to give me discounts at museums and on trains overseas. It never worked very well for discounts, although once it was enough to get me a teaching job in Fiji. He takes the card, holds it at arm's length for a better view of my photo, as if he's far-sighted.

"That you? Your hair's different here." I lean over and we both look at the picture together, trying to discern how different my hair was. Morticia looks also.

"Not really," I say. "Hardly at all. My hair was a little longer then maybe." Morticia agrees.

"Well, this could be forged." He tosses the card onto the counter. I notice the skin around his jowls hangs in unpleasant folds.

"Forged? Why would I forge this?"

"Why would I forge this?" he mocks, in an unnecessarily prissy version of my voice. My face is starting to get hot. I hate this man. There's definitely something wrong with him. "How much money are you taking into my country?" He emphasizes the "my" by drawing it out with an exaggerated southern accent. "Hey, guys! This should be good!" He says this loudly enough for his co-workers to hear but this time doesn't bother turning around so it's as if he's shouting this at us.

"Well, I have lots of money in my bank account and I'll be using this ATM card and my credit card. I could also show you..."

"Did you guys catch that?" he barks, still facing us.

"I could also show you my bank book. It's in the car." I pass him the bank cards.

He looks at each of the cards, turns them over, holds them at arm's length; he even sniffs them. Then, with an alarmingly vicious twist of his mouth, he says, "Oh, excuse me, I think these are plastic. Do these pieces of plastic look like money to you?" He pauses, waiting for an answer, and proceeds to do something bordering on the unforgivable. He tosses my two plastic cards up above the counter so they do little flips in the air, bounce down, and land on the floor.

"Of course they're plastic." I'd like this man to suffer a massive cardiac arrest, right here and now, I think as I bend down to retrieve my cards. "Haven't you seen credit cards before? What do you want? Travelers' checks? People don't need to use those anymore, not with ATMs everywhere. Do you want me to carry American cash across the border? What's the point of that when I can get it in five minutes at the nearest ATM around here? That's what everybody does."

"That's what everybody does," he mocks. "Did you guys hear that?" One of his co-workers seems to be taking a passing interest in this exchange. I look to this other man, exasperated, in hopes he'll add some sanity to the situation. He smiles slightly, shakes his head, and looks back to his computer screen. What's going on here? Why is this man not believing a word I say? Do I look like a criminal? And why is he picking on me alone while Morticia over here looks as if she's on her way to a satanic cult meeting. This guy's a complete bastard, an American Border Bastard. Mr. Border Bastard sighs deeply and says sternly, "I don't want you going into my country and running out of money. I don't want you on the street, young lady."

"On the street? What do I look like? A bum? A bag lady?" I take a step back, hold out my arms, look down at my shorts, purple top, and sandals. I don't think I look like a bum, not at all. In fact, I look like Mary Tyler Moore dressed for a summer day. "Do I? Do I look like a bum?" Both Mr. Border Bastard and Morticia look me over and seem to consider this. Despite Morticia's obvious sense of good fashion, she shakes her head. No, she doesn't think I look like a bum either. Is this man deranged? I want to ask him if he gets paid to be a jackass, if it's part of the job description. He's just waiting for me to blow up at him. I can feel it. He wants that. I decide to change tactics. I step back to the counter and look him in the eye. "Would it make a difference if I told you I were American?"

My words drop like lead. Mr. Border Bastard's face empties of expression. "Excuse me?" He cocks his head as if he didn't hear me right.

"I was born in the U.S., in Madison, Wisconsin. I have dual citizenship." I cringe when I say "dual citizenship" because from past experience at American borders I've learned they don't take kindly to that term.

The contours of his face begin to change. "Oh is that so? Is that so? Prove it." He folds his arms and stands up straight but this time doesn't shout anything back to the others.

I look through my wallet and hand him my birth certificate. He takes it without removing his eyes from mine. At first he just fingers it before taking a look, as if he knows the feel of counterfeit, then he turns it over, holds it at arm's length to read every word with his beady rat eyes. He frowns. He's unnerved, disarmed, furious.

"Why did you lie?"

"When?"

"You said you were Canadian. Did you not say you were Canadian?"

"I am Canadian, but I'm also American. Dual citizenship."

"What's that? We don't recognize dual citizenship here."

"Okay, fine. I'm American."

"Well, this will have to be checked. It could be forged like that teacher one." He puts the birth certificate down on the counter and doesn't seem to know what his next move should be.

"So can we go now?"

His face is actually flushed, as if he's lost his composure. "I can't stop you, young lady, from entering the United States at this point. I can't turn you back." He clears his throat.

I've really pissed him off. This is great. Since I'm free to go, I wonder if this is a good time to ask him if he was a member of Hitler Youth. He's a little young to have been an actual Nazi. Or perhaps his father was a Nazi and he grew up under a terrorist influence right here in Michigan. Both the U.S. and Canada let in all kinds of Nazis after the war. They thought Nazis could help in the fight against Communism. I'm wondering how to phrase the question when he says to me, "You can go, but who's your *Friday the 13th* friend over here?"

For the first time his attention is turned towards Morticia. Great. We've already been here forty-five minutes. A lurid light returns to his eyes as he looks over his new prey. He leans over the counter, feigning weariness. "And where are you going again? Chicago?"

"No, St. Louis." Morticia is actually beaming, perhaps anticipating meeting her Internet boyfriend at the mention of St. Louis. I'm amazed she can appear so calm in the face of such evil.

"Why on earth would you want to go there?"

"To visit a friend." She says this almost dreamily. She's serene. This is impressive.

"What kind of friend?"

"Just a friend. I have his address here." Morticia reaches into her knapsack to find her address book but he stops her before she shows it to him. Clearly he doesn't like the orderliness of this, her unruffled composure in the simple act of presenting an address which he fears will be there, neatly written on the white pages of a little book.

"Hold on there, Missy. First of all, how did you and this one over here meet?" He tilts his head in my direction but doesn't look at me. "What's the story with you two?"

We tell him about the ride board at the university.

"Well that's the biggest cock-and-bull story if I ever heard one."

This man is a cretin. I wait for him to shout something over his shoulder to the others but he must realize they aren't listening. He begins to grill Morticia about her financial situation and isn't satisfied that she has enough money to go to St. Louis. He asks her how long she's going to stay there to visit her so-called friend.

"Two weeks." She says this with the faintest expulsion of disheartened breath, as if two weeks can't possibly be long enough for what she'll encounter there.

"Aha. And how are you getting back to Canada? Is Miss California over here gonna come sweeping back from Hollywood to pick you up?"

"No, I'll take a train probably, or maybe my friend will drive me back. He wants to visit me in Canada."

"Get your story straight! You don't know how you're getting back?" He scrunches up his face into a knot. "What kind of a friend is this? Look here, young lady, if you want into the United States you're going to have to show me a train or a bus ticket exiting the United States, a ticket that leaves in nine days or less. You'll also have to show me an updated account of your financial situation. That's the only way I'm letting you in." He pauses, and for the first time we see his eyes widen to surprising proportions. "The ONLY way."

As one by one the words slither triumphantly from his mouth and coil inside me I realize that Mr. Border Bastard must be the keeper of some rare wickedness stored in a bitter heart. He's not a normal person. How can he do this to us? Now we have to go back across the bridge to Canada and drive all over the city of Sarnia to find a train or bus station and a branch of Morticia's bank. That could take hours. This is ludicrous. I look at Morticia and expect to see her as exasperated as I am. But, standing tall in her pagan outfit with her flowing shoe-polish black hair, Morticia, I mean Debbie!, is smiling at this horrid man, smiling as if she doesn't hate him, smiling from the depths of her pure free heart and glowing green eyes. I think this must be love that's doing this to Debbie. I think this must be life's blessing, that we can stare down the face of hatred any day of the week if we can write a letter to someone who will write us a letter back. Life's prayer for us is easy and everywhere in the world you find people who either listen or don't and everywhere in the world you find people who are crazy.

We leave Mr. Border Bastard officiously filling out some form, shaking his head in disgust as if he knows there's something we're hiding from him, some truth we haven't told. We cross back over the bridge to Canada and spend an hour going from train to bus station then back to the train station so Debbie can buy a return ticket from St. Louis. It's much more expensive doing it this way and she really was hoping to drive back with Alex instead of taking a train. When we get to a branch of her bank to request an updated statement of her entire bank account, Debbie is surprised to learn she has over fifteen thousand dollars in her account. For some reason her mother had deposited it without Debbie's knowledge. It seems Debbie is from a wealthy family. Fifteen thousand dollars should make Mr. Border Bastard happy, if happiness were possible for such a miserable excuse for a man.

Fortunately, we never find out what Mr. Border Bastard would have thought of Debbie's motherload of cash because we don't see him the second time we attempt to cross the border. The second time we attempt to cross the border, along with Debbie's return train ticket, updated bank statement, and our heated determination, another man is sitting at the immigration booth at the end of the bridge and this one looks different from the others. He doesn't have a military haircut and he's younger, seemingly more relaxed. "Of course he's probably just as mean as the others," I say to Debbie as we drive up to the white line. "Probably worse!"

"So where would you two be headed today?" He smiles, displaying a set of unnaturally white teeth. His uniform is starched. Ranger Smith comes to mind.

"St. Louis and California."

I hold my breath. Debbie thrusts out her documents, holds them steady in front of my face. I stare at the windshield, clenching the steering wheel.

"Have a good one."

I turn to him. "Excuse me?"

"A good one." He's smiling as if he's advertising Crest. His teeth actually glisten. What does he mean? Have a good what?

"Step on it! Go!" says Debbie.

"Go?"

"Go!"

I squeal the tires, not actually meaning to, but it feels right for the occasion. We're free. An incredible lightness takes over my body and everything around us—the highway and the sudden and numerous interstate signs, the duty-free store, the green grass on the boulevards, the ATM machines, the convenience stores, the blinding sun setting low on the horizon—feels like the hatching of a strange and marvelous dream. I'm allowed to be here. I'm American.

"Cool!" says Debbie. "Now I can put on some real makeup. I feel so naked like this."

Laurie Gough is the author of Kite Strings of the Southern Cross, *which won a silver medal from* Foreword *Magazine for Best Travel Book of the Year, and was short-listed for the Thomas Cook/Daily Telegraph Travel Book of the Year award in the U.K. She has also written for Salon.com,* Outpost, *and the* Toronto Globe and Mail. *Her work appears in several travel anthologies, including* A Woman's World, The Adventure of Food, Travelers' Tales Greece, Her Fork in the Road, *and* Sand in My Bra. *She lives in Quebec, Canada.*

CAM MCGRATH

Losing My Cool
in Calcutta

Serenity is hard to master in India.

DEMONSTRATIONS WERE BREAKING OUT ALL OVER THE CITY, and the Calcutta riot police were beating back the protesters with tear gas and billy clubs. I kept my distance from the melee, sticking to the back alleys as I made my way to the city center.

The trouble had started when the Joint Committee of Trade Unions in Banks, Insurance, and Financial Institutes (or J.C.T.U.B.I.F.I. for short) called a strike to protest bank privatization and payroll revision. As always in India, the strike had grown to include nearly a dozen other unions, everything from disgruntled postal workers to the rowdy Calcutta Seamsters Union.

Soon I was immersed in a frenzied mass of sweaty bodies. The impassioned river of discontent carried me as far as the main branch of the Reserve Bank of India, where protesters were throwing lumps of asphalt at a handful of security officers in front of the door. I slipped beneath an unfurled banner and liberated myself from the crowd.

I made my way to the American Express Office on Old Court House Road. The liberal sprinkling of asphalt nuggets near the entrance suggested that the protesters had already paid the office a visit, and I feared it would be closed. I needed it to be open. A week earlier, I had called my travel agent in the States to have her UPS an airline ticket to the office. I was to pick up the ticket at the office today, and fly home from Calcutta tomorrow.

But the Amex office was closed, a chain and padlock drawn across its door like a metal rosary. I went around the back of the building and banged on the delivery door. As I resigned to leave, the door swung open and a middle-aged gentleman greeted me.

"You are looking for American Express?"

"Yes, I thought you were closed."

"And we thought you were one of them," he said, alluding to the mob I had encountered earlier. "Please, come in quickly."

American Express offices around the world have a well-deserved reputation as bastions of efficiency in the midst of chaos. They provide a variety of useful services to travelers, including poste restante, and are generally more reliable and less chaotic than foreign banks and post offices. The air-conditioned Calcutta office was no exception. Despite the strike, it was staffed by a skeleton crew handling international accounts and general inquiries.

I explained my situation to the Amex mail clerk. He carefully searched the mail drawers for my ticket. Nothing. He searched again. Then he checked the manifest.

"I'm sorry sir, your mail has not arrived," he said sincerely.

My situation was looking bad. I had left all the ticketing arrangements to my travel agent, so I had no idea the airline, flight number, time, or route of my next day's flight. I called all the major airlines, but none had a booking under my name. I had to find that ticket!

"Is there a UPS office in Calcutta?" I asked the clerk.

"I think not, but perhaps there is a company that acts on their behalf. I suggest you check with the post office."

The helpful clerk gave me directions to the nearby post office, which was a large colonial building surrounded by an irate mob of picketing postal workers. Nevertheless, it was open, and only marginally more chaotic than usual. I shoved my way through the masses to the barred window marked General Enquiry, and hailed the clerk sipping tea behind the counter.

"Do you have a business directory or phone book I can use?" I asked.

"No. What are you looking for?"

"I need the address for United Parcel Service."

"No. I do not know the address."

"How can I find the address?"

He tilted his head, the Indian equivalent of a shoulder shrug.

"How would you find the address?" I persisted.

The clerk pointed to his co-workers, "I would ask him and him and him."

I couldn't help but wonder if somehow the four of them had memorized every address in Calcutta. The clerk asked around, but his co-workers only tilted their heads.

"No. We do not know that address. You must look in the phone guide."

"That's what I asked you for in the first place."

"No. You asked for a phone book," he replied smugly. "No matter. I do not have one anyway." He added that I might find a phone guide at the Central Telegraph Office nearby.

The Calcutta Central Telegraph Office was a warren of

offices housed in a decaying multi-story building. Employees idled behind monumental piles of paperwork, sipping tea and discussing whether or not they should strike. The Office of Information, a blatant misnomer, assured me that there was no current phone directory for Calcutta. Their representative explained that the entire Calcutta phone system was being revamped and numbers were changing daily.

"There is no current phone guide," he advised, "but you can call the information number."

"Information number?"

"Yes, of course," he said, obviously shocked by my ignorance. "Calcutta now has an information service. Dial 197."

I gestured to use the phone on his desk, but he apologized that it was, like most of the phones inside the Central Telegraph Office, not working today. He escorted me to the bank of yellow pay phones outside the building that he proudly touted as the most reliable public phones in Calcutta.

I approached the first phone and deposited a coin into the slot. One, nine, *clunk*. The number seven button fell through the panel. The next phone gave no dial tone, and two others appeared to have buttons missing. Of course all of the phones accepted coins, but none returned them—pay phones, it seems, are Calcutta's most reliable source of revenue.

I walked down the street in search of a private phone booth to make the call. Most of the strikers had retired to the shade as the midday sun had made the asphalt too sticky to throw. I found a call booth farther down the street and dialed the number for information.

"Information. *Namaste*," answered a lady.

"Hello. Do you speak English?"

"Yes, I speak perfectly good English," she replied a little irritated.

"Good. I am trying to find the phone number for United Parcel Service."

"United Park Service?" There was a short pause. "I do not have that number."

The glass booth felt like a blast furnace. Sweat streamed off my brow and soaked my shirt.

"United Parcel Service!" I shouted before the lady could hang up.

"What? United Bus Services?"

"No. Parcel, with the letter p. You know, l-m-n-o-p."

"Elementary?"

"No. Parcel, p-a-r-c-e-l."

"There is no such word," she replied curtly.

"Would you please check anyway."

She sighed and put me on hold. Beggars pressed their faces against the glass booth, extending their blackened hands through the doorway to tug on my shirt. "*Baksheesh! Baksheesh!* (Alms! Alms!)" Their chanting grew louder and louder, pushing my patience to the brink.

The lady returned. "No sir, there is no such company."

"What company?" I inquired suspiciously.

"United Elementary School."

I gritted my teeth. "Listen," I said articulating my words, "I want the phone number for United Parcel Service. Parcel—with a 'p' as in please."

"B as in beast?"

"No, p—it's the seventeenth letter in the goddamn alphabet!" I screamed as I lost my cool.

The lady paused, then responded firmly, "No, I am afraid you are mistaken, sir. The seventeenth letter in the goddamn alphabet is a q." She hung up.

I slammed the phone down, and upon recounting the

letters of the alphabet, bellowed in frustration. The beggars outside my booth roared with laughter. My actions only seemed to solidify their desire to harass me. "Meester! Meester!" They assailed me from all sides as I left the booth, provoking me if only to get a reaction. And I complied, flailing and gyrating halfway across Calcutta.

Sheer luck eventually led me to the office of Elbee Couriers, the Calcutta agent for UPS. With dogged persistence I convinced the staff to check their manifest for a package under my name. Nothing.

As evening approached in India and morning broke in the States, I managed to get a phone call through to my travel agent back home.

"I've got a big problem," I lamented. "The ticket for my flight tomorrow hasn't arrived."

"I'm so glad you called," she replied. "I had no way to reach you and tell you that I didn't send your ticket."

"What?"

"I figured there would be problems getting the ticket to you on time, so I booked a flight for you later next week. The ticket should arrive in two days. I hope you're not upset."

"Not really."

Cam McGrath's travels have taken him across Europe, Africa, Asia, and the Middle East. Now that he's cooled down a bit, he lives in the quieter chaos of Cairo, Egypt.

✦ ✦ ✦

Beijing Fish Tales

One bad, two good!

THE OLD MAN WORE A WIFE-BEATER TANK TOP AND TROUSERS rolled up to his kneecaps and carried a large cardboard box. Selecting a spot of sidewalk alongside a kid selling cleavers, he squatted into a position that would have taken an American man his age an hour to get out of and proceeded to unload five empty fishbowls. Then he looked up and beckoned me to join him. "*Qing lai.*"

Still inside the box was a tiny bowl crammed with so many goldfish, they swatted each other in the faces with their fins as they squirmed about. Suddenly, a black one pushed himself to the top of the heap and began to gasp frantically at the air, as if attempting suicide. He reminded me of the sad little porcupine I once saw being sold on the side of a similar Beijing road. The thought of buying the pitiable creature and liberating him in a forest didn't occur to me until he'd already been sold, and I sat up worrying about his culinary fate half the night. The time had come to make amends. Pointing at the suicidal fish, I told the old man, "*Wo yao!*" in Mandarin. I want!

Terrifically pleased, he scooped the fish out with a net and dunked him into one of the empty bowls. Then he tossed in a few friends.

"Wo yao yi ge!" I protested. I just want one.

"Yi ge—bu hao!" he chortled as he added another. One is bad.

"YI GE!" I repeated. Just one! I swiped his net and returned the impostors to their crowded bowl.

"Yi ge—bu hao!" he insisted, as he re-seized the net and threw them back in. One is bad.

This carried on for quite some time, but at last I escaped with *yi ge*, whom I named Xiao He, or Little River. My lunch break nearly over, I headed back to *China Daily*—the newspaper where I worked at the time—and crossed paths with some schoolchildren wearing identical blue sweatsuits and bright yellow caps. When I bent down to show them my new pet, the leader of the pack—a nine-year-old with buck teeth and braids—grimaced. Holding her index finger high in the air, she chirped: *"Yi ge—bu hao!"* One is bad.

I pushed her aside and continued along the street. What did little kids know about aquatic life?

As I entered my office beaming like a new mother, my colleague Mao Lan rushed over and peered into the bowl excitedly. Her exuberance instantly evaporated.

"You only bought one. Where are his friends?" she asked, her big eyes widening with alarm.

"I'm his friend."

"No, you're not. You're different."

"He wants some privacy."

"No, he doesn't. He's Chinese."

"He's American now!"

She walked away muttering: *"Yi ge—bu hao!"* One is bad.

After work, I took Xiao He home with me. As we walked through the gate, a security guard strolled over to see what was inside the bowl. "Why did you only buy one?" he asked, his brows crinkled with concern.

"He is an American fish."

"*Shi ma?*" Really?

"*Shi.*" Then I carried Xiao He up four flights of stairs to his new flat, careful not to slosh his water out. He didn't come with instructions, so I improvised, feeding him three times a day like Dad did me, filling his bowl with marbles and plastic action figures, and letting him swim around the bathtub each night to stretch out his fins. I even left the radio on during the day so he wouldn't get bored. But within a few days, Xiao He started getting lethargic. My friends came over to diagnose his paling scales.

"He's lonely!" Yuer said.

"He's homesick!" Liu said.

"He misses his friends!" my language tutor said.

By the following afternoon, Xiao He had turned almost translucent. Thinking him dirty, I tossed him in the bathtub and scrubbed out his bowl. As soon as he returned to his sparkling home, however, he coughed twice and floated belly-up to the top. I sighed and flushed him down the toilet.

Just then, someone knocked at the door. It was a cleaning attendant, coming to collect the trash.

"Where's your fish?" she pointed at the empty bowl.

"*Ta si le.*" He died.

"*Si le?*" she repeated, her slender fingers reaching into the bowl and stroking his toys. Then she wiped her hands briskly and walked out the door with my trash.

"*Yi ge—bu hao!*" she declared before slamming it shut.

＊

Stephanie Elizondo Griest has belly-danced with Cuban rumba queens, mingled with the Russian Mafia, and edited the propaganda of the Chinese Communist Party. These adventures are the subject of her first book: Around the Bloc: My Life in Moscow, Beijing, and Havana *and are available at www.aroundthebloc.com. She has also written for* The New York Times, Washington Post, Latina Magazine, *and* Travelers' Tales Cuba, Travelers' Tales Turkey, *and* Her Fork in the Road. *She once drove 45,000 miles across the nation in a beat-up Honda, documenting alternative U.S. history for a website for kids at www.ustrek.org on a $15 daily budget.*

BENNETT STEVENS

Snap Happy and the Nagas

*A freelance photographer in India
goes with the flow.*

FIVE DAYS PRIOR TO MAUNI AMAVASYA, THE MOTHER OF ALL
Kumbha Mela bathing days, the district High Court in
Allahabad decreed that ALL photography was banned within
500 meters of any *sangam* (sacred confluence of rivers). This
was the worst news possible for anyone with a serious camera, with the lone exception of NASA, who had agreed that
*the single largest gathering of humanity the planet Earth has ever
known,* was worth orbiting over for a snap or two.

I heard the court's reasoning three ways: 1) That Channel
4, during some of its broadcasts back to the UK, had shown
Indian women with exposed breasts bathing in the holy
sangam and had therefore made mockery of the Hindu religion for purposes of monetary gain via high ratings. This on
its face was patently ridiculous. Even if such occasions did
occur on Channel 4 broadcasts, they would likely have had
just the opposite effect. Trust me when I tell you that the
quality of breasts exposed in the *sangam* were not anything
anyone wants to see, not even an Englishman. 2) That a

Western photographer was seen *aiming his lens* in the direction of a pair of Indian breasts in the throes of watery worship. Good heavens. 3) That a Western woman, carried away not by devotion but by drugs and raving sacrilege, stripped herself nude and frolicked through the *sangam*, again making mockery of the Hindu religion, as slavering photographers snapped her every frolic.

The first two possible reasons were in the Allahabad papers and widely circulated on a grapevine of slowly shaking heads and incredulous smiles. The last one I heard from an AFP cameraman two months later in Phnom Penh. In any event, or even in the event of all three, the decision to ban cameras would prove short-sighted, virulent, and typically Indian— God bless all billion of 'em. "Small fire is best being extinguished with petrol" might as well be the national motto.

The first proof of virulence—and casualty—came immediately. An Indian cameraman was set upon with a cane for shooting near the *sangam* and had his camera confiscated by an army officer. He was justifiably furious and took his case immediately to the Media Center—an assemblage of drab, uninspired tents and equally drab and uninspired bureaucrats seemingly assembled for the sole purpose of doing nothing at all constructive.

A heated debate ensued, resulting first in the photographer's camera being smashed to the ground, and second, with his head being smashed with a brick. A media protest was later organized and a demonstration took place outside the Media Center, resulting, predictably, in nothing at all constructive.

Despite dire warnings of the inevitable chaos to come, the High Court stood firm. Now you had a case of photographers and camera crews from all over the world having gone to a lot of effort and expense to be here—some even at the behest of the Indian government—being told they could not do what they came here to do, which was, ostensibly, something constructive.

Now it was all starting to make sense, because, after all, we were in India.

Everybody I spoke with was irked but undeterred. Channel 4 was going with hidden cameras. So were the Japanese and even some of the Indian crews. A Dutch group of still photographers was going to try and man the tower about 600 meters from the *sangam* with high-powered lenses. Kadeem and other videographers were going to try their luck in a rowboat. Other still-snappers like Mac (demi-famed Aussie photographer Alastair McNaughton) and myself were tucking our cameras under our clothes and taking our chances. So basically, what you had was 10,000 Indian Army men going into battle against a couple of hundred miscreants with cameras hiding amidst millions upon millions of devout civilians. Though the army had in possession a wide array of death-causing devices, canes, praise Vishnu, were to be the weapon of choice.

With all those millions of people and all those square miles of *mela* grounds, you'd think your odds as a photographer of going undetected were pretty good. That is until you took in the other factors. The target area on this day was comparatively small—the twenty- to thirty-meter wide, two-kilometer long procession route that would carry the *mela's* main attraction, those zany Naga Babas, down to bathe in the Naga section of the main *sangam*. That was it. This was Ground Zero. Another factor not to be overlooked: that of being a foreigner. We stood out in this crowd like a rainbow in *Pleasantville*. Add a camera to that, which you had to take out sometime, and you morphed into the aurora borealis. The pilgrims knew about the camera ban and believing the hyperbolic papers, many among them would consider us a scurrilous enemy to piety on this, the greatest day of their religious lives.

Five thousand four hundred and sixty-five years after the first *Mauni Amavasya*, observed by that unnamed nudist proto-astronomer in 3464 B.C., marks not only the origins of the Kumbha Mela, but also the Naga Babas as "proto-origi-nators." To this day the thirteen *akharas* of the Shambhu Panch, led by the infamous Juna Akhara, determine exact bathing dates and throw a lot of weight around this very heavy happening.

The night before Mac and I settled in for cocktail hour at Camp Pilot Baba and discussed our camera ban battle plan. Black rum and reverse osmosis Ganga water (to purify it of burnt body parts, et al.), stirred not shaken, served in thimble-sized plastic *chai* cups of a thickness comparable to Saran Wrap, was the best we could do. We had two plans to consider, and neither included obeying the High Court. Plan A was to make our way down to the main *sangam* area where the Grand Procession and the Nagas would dump out into the rivers' confluence. There we would stake out a vantage point behind the lines, cameras hidden, and hope for the best. But the drawbacks didn't excite us—no front-row advantages afforded by the media corral that lined the route, not to mention the burgeoning slew of other cameramen and photographers all trying to stay invisible while vying for position. There was the distinct possibility of being left walking away with a squat named Diddly.

Plan B, as befitting the nature of Plan B's everywhere

would be more risky but the payoff was potentially far greater. It meant walking right under the vigilant eyes of that pesky, ubiquitous Indian Army and millions of pilgrims on high camera alert. We would attempt to walk right smack in the middle of the Grand Procession, right inside the Juna Akhara. And keep every available appendage crossed.

Plan B it was.

The decision made, we had a few more plastic thimbles of rum, did ritual *puja* to Shiva, and Mac regaled the night with war stories from the far flung reaches of the globe, all thematic and inspirational to the snapper's never ending mystic quest for—*the shot*.

The inner circle of devotees, seventy-five or so, which included half a dozen Westerners, made their way from Pilot Baba's compound to the Juna Akhara camp beginning about midnight. That meant about five hours of sitting around shivering in the darkest before the dawn and the start of the Grand Procession. No thank you please. We slept in until four A.M. It was neither a good sleep nor an easy rise. It was still freezing. And there was rumbling and foreboding.

In anticipation of the rumbling's release, I cleared Mac out of the tent and ran to wave the white flag at the bad *sabji* jihad that had been firing mortar rounds around my intestines for the last forty-eight hours. Actually, jihad was a poor choice of metaphors, for what then passed from me— with extreme prejudice—had more of a Vesuvius-like quality. The staccato bursts of molten green *sabji* that erupted from the bowels of my bowels were so loud and so ridiculous that I couldn't help but laugh out loud. When I thought about all the bleary eyed Indians in nearby tents waking to the magnitude of this magma melody, accompanied by the disjointed guffaws of an obviously mad foreigner—I got hysterical.

But I wasn't the least bit happy about it, let me tell you.

The army's mindset was clear at the outset. If they thought you didn't look like you belonged wherever it was that you were, you were beaten somewhere you did. With a cane. We had just slid into the Juna Akhara seconds before the cavalry blocked it off. As we stood inside, nervous and unsure as to the status of our belonging, we watched two men get thrashed out of the Akhara. This was a cause for concern. We'd been there enough times though, had hung around and let it be known to anyone who would listen—however technically untrue—that we were part of our Rolex guru's personal media team, and this, apparently, was enough to make us look like we belonged.

The Juna Akhara is considered the most fierce and individualistic of the thirteen *akharas*, still adhering to and practicing many of the more ancient rites, rituals, and *tapasayas*. They are a Shaiva sect but their present deity is Dattatreya, a partial incarnation of rival deity Vishnu, with many Shiva characteristics. Only in recent years did the kinder, gentler Dattatreya replace Bhairava, who is depicted in a multi-headed perpetual ecstasy, surrounded by a bevy of hot Hindu babes, slugging wine, fornicating like a mad sultan, and eating flesh from a human skull.

Though it is clear the Juna hierarchy has seen the future of their existence as dependent on a certain level of Hindu-style political correctness that includes a manipulative openness to the media, it is just as clear that certain minority factions within its ranks do not welcome these changes. The problem is, you never know who these "skull munching" faction members are until they reveal themselves, and these revelations are never pleasant.

In light of this—even with the general mood within the *akhara* one of positive excitement, with plenty of laughing and hand warming over *dhunni* fires, passing of the *charas chillum*, *asana* practice, and rolling naked through holy ash—we thought it best to mingle into the relative security of the Pilot Baba retinue.

In stark contrast to the mood inside, outside the *akhara,* where our immediate futures lay, was a different story. There is a certain tension that accompanies incessant cop whistles punctuated with the occasional crisp crack of cane. The brute smell of testosterone was in the air. No, this wasn't war, and barring some terrorist siege or stampede, not even life or death. But it was battle, and bodily injury and destruction of equipment was possible, and it did weigh on us. Perhaps worse and weighing more heavily, at least on me as a relative rookie, was the very real possibility in all this mayhem of being denied position to get *the shot*. I didn't come all this way and go through all this shit to get shut out.

As we stood around and shivered waiting for things to get started, wouldn't you know it, "Vesuvius" began rumbling again. Its molten dissonance obviously hadn't been exhausted during its most recent pyrotechnics back at camp. Rather than seek out the *akhara* squatter however, I decided to cinch up and bear it.

The assassins of aesthetics and proper pomp—the tractors and the attached steroidal Radio Flyers that would serve in lieu of the elephants and chariots of the past—had been earlier fitted with the Shaiva red thrones trimmed in gold that would frame the gurus, shaded with red umbrellas hung with gold tassels, and festooned with garlands of marigolds enough to endanger the species. We had been standing around for about forty-five minutes when the tractors roared to life and a line of *nagas* (naked, ash-smeared madmen wielding medieval weaponry) came running onto the sandy boulevard where the procession had begun to take form. We followed them out, sticking close to our protective pod of devotees carrying the same pennants and banners emblazoned with the black bearded image of Pilot Baba, our now-beardless master, and more importantly, as a major player in the Juna Junta, our protector.

As the light of dawn crept into the sky, the "chariots" began to fill with honored guests and hierarchy, stacking themselves in around the thrones of their masters thick as French fries in extra-large red and gold containers. In the procession line we again did our best to act like we belonged. This consisted entirely of looking for all the world like we didn't, which of course came naturally. As if to press home the point, a white-uniformed brass band ambled right up to us and began belting out utterly unrecognizable, and to our ears, utterly un-rhythmical swaths of brassy, pounding sound that seemed to scream, "You don't belong here!"

Paranoid? Perhaps. Justifiably so? Damn straight.

But never mind all that. What happened to our *nagas*? We'd lost them. Just how one manages to lose thousands of *nagas* I don't know, but we had. Just where they had gone we would be able to surmise shortly.

Make no mistake about it, to the *akharas* (and all the other thousand-plus sects present as well) the modern Kumbha Mela is the greatest religious recruitment boon since loaves and fishes. With rare exception, all new prospective *akhara* members are initiated at one Kumbh or another, every three years. Naturally it is "being extra most auspicious" as one sadhu told us, to receive initiation during the rare Maha Kumbh, the one we were smack in the midst of, which ends a 144-year cycle. Or begins one. I never did get it straight. Regardless of the level of auspiciousness, of the upwards of 3,000 who receive initiation at each Kumbha Mela, fewer than 10 percent stick around long enough to see the next batch of recruits get their heads shaved and *shikas* lopped off. Evidently, a life lived naked and unemployed, spending summers meditating with cow-dung fires on your head is not as easy as it might first appear.

"Here they are!" decreed Mac. "Our nutters..."

And there they were, our nutters, streaming and screaming right past us with a fresh batch of nutters in tow (Vaishnavas), evidenced by the single rupee-sized patches of hair left on their shaven heads, the last vestiges of their guru-shorn *shikas*. They emptied into a semi-circle just ahead of us, where several veterans, easily identified by their unfurled, knee-length *jatas*, began whirling swords and battle axes in a semi-skillful display of martial artistry. Some of this I was able to capture on video just before a bit of brazen adumbration befell me.

Some perfect asshole, here affirming the Asshole-in-Every-Crowd Theory, appeared from nowhere, struck down fiercely upon my pack and tried to grab my camera shouting—ever so distinctly and succinctly—"No photo!" At least he was to the point. As much as I would like to have ripped him an expansive new orifice befitting his station in life, I did the smart thing instead, saying nothing and immediately spiriting away into the crowd. He did not pursue, as is always the case with these Assholes in Every Crowd. At least in India. It works with Indian cops and soldiers too. Usually.

I was rattled a bit, not wanting to be exposed and thrown out before this "function" for 30 million even began. As the

Grand Procession started to roll shortly thereafter, the great babas all ensconced in their thrones surrounded by VIP devotees, I made my way back near the front where Mac and the pod were. Quite matter of fact Mac said, "You should have left that bloody video contraption behind." He was right of course. Under these conditions one had to get his shot and get it quick. The video camera was a burden and a risk, but I couldn't bring myself to leave it.

We shrunk into the middle of our now-chanting pod of belonging and began the march, taking care to keep our big, guilty-looking white heads from jutting too far above the others. All told there were about 1,000 *nagas* and initiates ahead of us and another thousand behind, but that's just a guess. The entire length of the procession, which included all thirteen *akharas* and their farm equipment, stretched back as far as I could see. It would take nearly three hours to complete. Being near the front, however, where the real action was, meant we would do it in something under an hour.

The army was positioned everywhere along the route. Indians who dared enter the procession or even stepped towards it were routinely thrashed back with canes. Whistles curdled the air, even piercing through the horns, the drums, and the chanting. Soldiers glared in at us routinely and when they did, they saw two shrinking white men crudely lip-synching chants in Hindi. The #5 pontoon bridge over the Ganga which we now approached would mark the next crucial stage. Soldiers clustered near the entrance, some on horseback, and the procession line would have to narrow considerably in order to file onto the bridge, exposing us further. No soldiers were on the bridge, however, and if we made it on we'd be free to shoot and enjoy the ride. Until the other side anyway, where another cluster of menace awaited.

Feeling more naked than our *naga* cohorts, we nevertheless squeezed through and onto the crossing safely.

It was there we were able to take in the enormity of the crowd gathered to watch the procession (us!) and to bathe along the east bank of the Ganges. A thick kaleidoscopic expanse of pilgrims stretched into the distance past the highway and railway bridges, as far as the eye pressed to a 320x digital zoom could see. It was an amazing rush to be in the middle of it all, the energy sweeping the angst away like a cosmic Bissel. Now that I'd deciphered the words, I was genuinely moved to join in the chanting: "*Har! Har! Maha Dev! Har! Har! Maha Dev!*" It was a grand and glorious release, arms raised like a victorious Caesar returning to Rome, right there in front of *the single largest gathering of humanity the planet Earth has ever known.*

We made it easily past the "cluster of menace" on the other side. Two hundred meters of chanting later we made the left turn that led down to the main *sangam*, perhaps another five hundred meters beyond. At this point the procession split in two with the *nagas* to the left and everybody else to the right. There the rest of the *nagas* caught up and paired up—marching two-by-two the final leg towards the Kumbha Mela's Big Splash Moment, holding hands and yelping and stabbing at the heavens with *trishuls*, cutlasses, and battle axes.

By this time we had managed to snap a few shots each, but they had a perfunctory feel for me, taken more for the act than the result. This was the kind of difficult light and building, noisy action that begged for video, which I was managing to steal a bit of as well. I was thrilled, as I knew nobody else was in any kind of position to get the video I was getting. That is until I took in the incongruous sight of an especially maniacal-looking *naga* sporting a Panasonic Hi8, freely immortalizing his naked brethren's march towards the waters of *moksha*. I felt strangely slighted, but also thought: "Why didn't I think of that?" A Rasta wig, a *trishul*, a little ash smearing, a whole lotta naked and…"

And this is where it all began to go terribly wrong.

My photo envy got the best of me; there was just no way I was going to be outdone by some prehistoric, hash-laced heathen with inferior equipment. Right on cue, another "illegal" photographer suffering perhaps the same pangs of envy I was, stepped into the no-man's land between the marching *nagas* and us, and started snapping. He was soon set upon, not by a soldier, but by one of the additional security personnel in faded orange robes employed specifically to keep processional order. These guys were thugs in turbans, who went to the cane even faster than the soldiers did. This particular thug, however, quite un-thug like, held his cane and lashed the man severely by means of tongue and larynx only.

"Is that the only price I have to pay?" I can take a tongue lashing with the best of them if I have to. The photographer returned freely from whence he came. Next thing I remember I, the great idiot, was out in no-man's land myself, face glued about a second too long over the video eyepiece.

CRACK!

Blindsided by a cane across the trapezium, followed by a death grip seizing down from behind and onto the video camera, trying to wrest it away. I held on for all I was worth, instinctively bending forward and spreading out my base so as not to be brought down and—in all that strain—Vesuvius let loose.

It was not a major eruption and no villages would have to be evacuated, but it was of sufficient force to cause serious blight across the back forty of an otherwise pristine pair of olive green trousers. It could have been worse. I mean, for example, I could have just shat myself in front of *the single largest gathering of humanity the planet Earth has ever known!*

As if this weren't obscenely more than enough, my two assailants forced me back through the procession line, pod bodies parting in mortal dread, and crashing into the cruel irony of the empty media corral. The thug was still trying with all his might to tear the camera from my desperate grip. For me, the camera represented the last shred of dignity I had and there was just no way that he was gonna get it. I'd sooner we ripped the thing in half. For some reason no attempt was made on my 35mm Nikon, which just hung and swung in the ruckus, refusing to get involved.

With the thug still gripping my camera and the soldier whacking me with his cane with one hand while pushing me with the other, they forced me *through* the fence and into the media corral. There, waiting to get in on the fun stood another soldier, cane at the ready.

WHACK!

I had seen it coming and lurched forward just in time. He had struck the thug. Small victory. I struggled down the corral determined to get away, pulling the thug, who was really starting to become a nuisance, by the camera with me. They tried now to shove me through the fence on the other side, into the crowd of pilgrims, but I wanted none of that. I just kept boring forward at an increasing clip hoping they'd abandon me, like these types always had before but wouldn't now. Finally we wrestled to an exhausted stop in front of a gawking throng of pilgrims no longer paying any attention at all to the procession. A parade stands no chance against good, live-action toilet humor and a good thrashing. I immediately launched into a colorful bit of hyperbole, professing my innocence as the official photographer of the Juna Akhara and Pilot Baba and my right to be let back into the procession, where I *belonged*, shit pants and all. They responded by continuing to thrash and shout at me in a Gatling-gun hail of gibberish. I was getting nowhere but further humiliated and chose, choicelessly, to acquiesce. I bent to duck through the fence into the crowd and was kindly assisted with a parting blow to the shoulder and a jack-booted stomp to the calf.

Walking away my attackers were laughing like jackals after a hyena kill, presumably, at the jackass who just shat himself in front of *the single largest gathering of humanity the planet Earth has ever known!*

I could smell it now. Was that me? Squatting to hide my shame, battered and bleeding on my cameras, I looked back at the crowd that held me captive against the fence. They were sitting in the sand, twenty rows deep and standing another ten behind. All eyes, wide and white and dark in the middle, were on me. What a fucking nightmare. I struggled to take off my sweatshirt and tie it by the arms around my waist to hide my shame. The woman nearest me, who was breastfeeding her baby, glared at me like I'd just gutted a cow with a *trishul*. Even her baby took time out from its suckling to give me a look of such seeming disgust that, coming from a baby, was not only strangely disconcerting but—gauging from the smell—the height of hypocrisy. I was disconcerted enough without getting shit from some hypocrite infant.

I really had to get out of there. Pressing matters to attend to. But how? There was not an inch of space anywhere to be had in this sea of saris, turbans, and nose rings. What could I do but stand up and take the first step? They could either move or get stepped on. Or worse, sat on. They made way, and I stumbled through.

Once free I started walking fast, hoping nothing slid down my leg as I scanned the land for the corrugated-tin sheeting that semi-privatized the squat-hole toilets. There were supposed to be 74,000 of them spread everywhere around the *mela* grounds. Everywhere, of course, but where I was. I was beginning to think this just wasn't my day.

My worst fear (well, previous worst fear) as a photographer on the world's biggest stage had been realized. I would not in any way, shape, manner, or form, be in position to get *the shot.*

After all I'd been through, of all things to have happen, this! Had I but practiced a few minutes more of Mac-like professional patience I'd have been there shooting with him.

With clean pants.

The big red cross ahead marked a welcome sight—a hospital camp. I thought it might offer a more private, possibly more upscale option for my squat-holing pleasure. I would be wrong. I should have learned not to think by then. My bleeding hands along with the newly discovered bleeding bridge of my nose qualified me for immediate entry. At first they said there was no toilet and insisted I get treatment for my wounds. I protested, they insisted, I protested some more, they insisted some more, I untied my sweatshirt and pointed out the disposition of my ass, and they pointed out the disposition of the corrugated-tin squat hole off in the corner, which to me in that moment was Shangri-fucking-la.

But the nightmare was not quite over. This episode had an uncanny way of getting stranger and stranger. The decidedly low-scale, decidedly un-private squat hole had been in recent use. There was no water. What there was, set smartly against the white porcelain urine channel that led into the hole, was a huge swirl of steaming shit—the perfect shit—looking for all the world like a Dairy Queen ice cream dispenser had been summoned from hell to squeeze it there for the sole purpose of further fucking with my mind. It stood so high and well balanced that The Man With the Dairy Queen Sphincter must have had to gently rise and slowly rotate himself with a laser-like precision rarely found amongst mere mortals. A fun-loving dung beetle could have run the spiraling ledge from bottom to top with nothing to break his stride save sheer exhaustion. So skilled was this fecal craftsman, so attuned to the universe was he, that left crowning this monument to the gastrointestinal tract was an impossibly delicate, thrice curling creamy pigtail—the final artistic flourish of a scatological masterwork. What an anus! It was so damned perfect it bordered on the miraculous, the highest manifestation of the lowest order. Looking back on it now, I really should have photographed it. I mean, who knows, maybe I'd been in position to get *the shot* after all.

I waddled out to fill the water jug. It just never ends in India. Everybody in the compound, including those tending to patients and the patients themselves, watched me fill the jug. I was beyond caring. As the water pounded into the clay jug, my mind kept repeating Mac's fateful words over and over: "You should have left that bloody video contraption behind…should have left that bloody…"

Back in the relative privacy of my squat hole, the masterwork turd mocking me all the while, I cleaned myself with the now wet and unsoiled front section of my own Mervyn's 3-for-$12 boxer shorts. I have never felt such utter defeat. I just *knew* Mac was down at the *sangam* getting the shots, I knew it! Not out of any supernatural intuitiveness on my part, but because I had learned through personal experience how the universe worked, at least for me, and the point of my lesson just wouldn't have been driven home hard enough had Mac somehow been foiled.

Yes-sir-ee, ole Snap Baba was down there snapping away all right, filling his ancient Nikon with images of wild-eyed *nagas* splashing around ululating like—well—*nagas*. Nobody and I mean nobody, splashes and ululates like they do. This of course is exactly where I should have been, would have been, if not for my own lapse in awareness and the intelligent application of just a *little* more patience.

Bright side? Anti-climatic perhaps, but yes, there was indeed a bright side. Two of them in fact. First, I was pretty confident I now had something to write about that nobody else could, or would, even if they could. Second, the extra mesh liner the good people who make Exofficio trousers had provided proved the crucial difference in reducing the out-wardly visible signs of my unfortunate discharge into a single, egg-sized ovoid. This was more than just easily cleaned; it was a show of divine mercy for which I am eternally grateful. My eruptive, splattery splendor had been nowhere near as noticeable to the *single largest gathering of*—as I had feared.

It truly is, the little things.

Bennett Stevens is a screenwriter, bartender, and complete idiot who, by 1999, had reached the pinnacle of his decline. It was at this point that he finally decided to pack up and chase his dream of becoming a world-culture photographer, and has been stumbling and stealing souls across this wobbly orb ever since. He is based in Bangkok, Thailand.

Hungry?

Sometimes a man just needs a chicken.

WHEN I SAW A SIGN INSIDE A SHOPPING MALL SOMEWHERE off the beaten path in Southeast Asia that said "Kenny Rogers' Roasters," I was intrigued, but skeptical. I had never heard of such a place; it might be a music store, it might be a hair salon, but it was going to be worth a look.

In Southeast Asia, you have to be skeptical of brand names because of all of the trademark infringement. Even though the Levi's you just bought for $9 have the little red tag and buttons that say Levi's, they give a whole new meaning to "The Original." I opened the door. I saw a picture of Kenny on the wall, but I needed to see what the place really was. It looked like a restaurant, that was enough for me.

I had been in Asia just over two months, something like ten weeks, or if you're counting days, about seventy. Of course, if you're counting meals, like I am, think about two hundred and ten. Add iodine-purified water, a permanent layer of dust on my tongue, and let's just say that I couldn't even hold down the food that I do eat and it was safe to declare that food was becoming my meaning, my passion. I dreamt up meals in my head: leafy salads, slippery pastas, anything without rice and noodles. Oh, and add six months of Africa where they specialized in *sadza* and cassava. Sure, it sounded exotic and adventurous, but at this point given a choice between a baked potato and the Great Wall of China…pass the sour cream.

Rice and noodles, rice or noodles, fried, fried with egg, with fish sauce, curry sauce, tomato sauce, with vegetable oil, peanut oil, just plain yellow oil, with beef, chicken, pork, "You need fork?" It didn't matter what was listed on the menu, you were going to get rice. Noodle soup, rice wine, rice whiskey. You didn't even need to be in a restaurant. "You like tour today, mistah? To rice paddies!" It was a conspiracy. "Rice with crap?" I pointed to a menu listing. "Seefoo, mistah!"

I stepped inside the Kenny Rogers place and immediately the perfume of a non-rice, non-noodle food paralyzed me like nerve gas, but good nerve gas. I struggled to move forward, slowed by skepticism and the fear of denial, or worse, the clarity of my own hallucinations. I tried to place the smell and, *boom*, I had it: my cousin's kitchen on Thanksgiving Day. Turkey, gravy, mashed potatoes. My mouth curved into a delirious smile. I didn't even know Kenny cooked.

In southern Africa, Malawi specialized in a leafy vegetable called cassava that was a hybrid of cabbage and papier-mâché. Great for vegetarians with broken bones, make a little salad and pack the rest around your fractured elbow, sit out in the sun to dry.

In a remote hilltop village I sat on the verandah of my colonial-style guesthouse and watched the sunset after a day's hike up the mountain. The owner asked me if I would like to eat; I said that I would. She had the courtesy to get right to the point, all they had was rice and cassava. They were the only place in the village. I had rice and cassava for the next four days. And nights.

I finally got my hands on some chicken in a nearby town called Chitimba. Tough, dry, and muscular, characteristics worthy of a body-guard, not a chicken. I took a peek at the chicken coroner report. Cause of death: old age.

There was a picture on the wall of a woman who was apparently Kenny Rogers's wife. People waited with trays behind a glass counter. Steam rose from different areas and I moved in closer. I had a strange feeling in my mouth, pasty and dry, and I licked my lips slowly. My taste buds called out, in a million wimpy prisoner voices, "Help. Help."

I stood in front of the glass counter and rubbed my eyes because I truly didn't believe them. As if I had uncovered ancient artifacts after years of digging, my eyes widened and my jaw dropped as the scene before me was too great for my mere mortal comprehension. It had been too long, I just didn't believe it anymore. I closed my eyes and hoped.

Of course there were a few other choices back in Africa, but it's the whole real traveler thing, when in Rome and doing as the Romans and all. But I had been doing as the goddamn Romans for so long that the Italian government should award me an honorary passport. The thought of Rome was sounding pretty good about now as a matter of fact: lasagna, pesto, cute little butterfly pastas dripping in a creamy white sauce, an Italian waitress with long, dark hair in a tight white T-shirt and jeans and sandals, maybe fresh bread, maybe melted butter, maybe I should stop traveling. Oh, fresh bread. I could almost taste the butter on my tongue, warm and tangy, slippery and oily, the waitress might smile at me, might give me extra butter. I wasn't going to make it through another four months in Asia.

I opened my eyes and looked through the plate glass and saw baked potatoes snuggled next to each other under hot lamps, soaking up the warm rays. Real baked potatoes. My eyes drifted to the right: bins of shiny green peas, creamy white sauces, thick and brown gravy, red and luscious tomato sauce. Thoughts were flying through my head that I hadn't put there, visions of passionate and even violent eating that was nothing human, nothing of my own doing. My stomach jumped up and kicked my heart: forget love, this was lust. Ears of corn lay nestled together in a liquid bed of warm butter, snuggled next to each other cozy and sweet. I felt something on the side of my chin and instinctively wiped it with the back of my hand. Drool.

For six months in Africa I stared into plates of a pasty mashed-potato looking substance called sadza. *Actually, comparing it to mashed potatoes is giving it too much credit as mashed potatoes actually have taste.* Sadza *is more of a tool. The locals scoop up a bit in their hands and then use it as a sort of Velcro napkin to pick up other items on their plate and then eat the item and the napkin. Actually, a napkin is probably closer in taste.*

Back in Kenny's kitchen, from each tub of delight rose a visible perfume of snaking steam, genies rising out of bottles, they twisted and turned in the air and made their way directly into my nostrils and lifted me off the ground. A forest of dark green broccoli sat so near a tub of oozing, bubbling, thick and rich creamy cheese sauce that I knew that they longed for each other, they needed to be together, it was their destiny, and I would make it happen. A hunger rose from my belly and went through my body like electricity, but slowly and it felt good, real good. I shuddered.

Waves of mashed potatoes whipped up high like a stormy sea, little tide pools of butter shimmered in delight, and finely chopped chives waited innocently next to the storm. Soft clouds of snow white sour cream floated in a cool tin bin. I felt faint, I swayed in my sandals. I struggled to swallow. I heard a strange smacking sound, but soon realized that it came from

my own mouth. I was licking my lips like a lion. My body was
doing things that I only noticed after some time. I was losing
control. I closed my eyes again, attempting to calm down.

*Some five months earlier on the northern border of Malawi near
Tanzania, after a long day on trains, buses, and mini-vans, I spotted
a small restaurant called Mexico. My hopes and dreams went
through the roof as images of tacos, enchiladas, and fresh corn tortillas
rushed the stage of my mind like rock concert fans. I chatted with the
owner as I looked over the menu. I didn't really recognize anything
Mexican. I asked him why he named his restaurant Mexico. He
beamed a huge friendly African smile and said in a thick accent and
in all honesty, "I don't know!" In fact, there was nothing even re-
motely Mexican about the place. I ordered fried rice and chicken. The
friendly waitress scurried off to the kitchen only to quickly return to
tell me that there wasn't any chicken tonight. I looked up and down
the long menu on the wall, full of yummy sounding dishes, and made
another selection. She scurried away, returned. Nope, sorry. I chose
again, she came back. I looked up at the menu and calculated that
this could only happen another seven times, but I decided to make
the bold move and asked, "What DO you have?" "Rice and cassava." My head dropped heavily. Welcome to Africa.*

Again my eyes opened and I felt stable. Then I looked
down. A tar pit of black beans bubbled and I could taste each
one individually if only my tongue could taste what my eyes
could see. I started to stick out my tongue, just to see if it
could extend another three feet, but I caught myself, hoping
no one was watching. I didn't know if I had been standing
there for two minutes or two hours or if I was standing there
at all. It couldn't all be true, not all together in one place. I
wanted to look at the other people in the restaurant, to see if
they were real, to see if they took trays, paid money, and then
feasted like kings, but I couldn't turn my head.

A fear suddenly came over me that maybe it was all an overly cruel and terribly realistic Larium dream, my friendly hallucinogenic anti-malaria drug. I was stuck behind the glass plate, bulletproof no less, handcuffed to barrels of rice and noodles while naked nymphs licked creamy sauces from the valleys of each other's navels, tore at succulent spare ribs with the violence of hyenas, sauce dripping from their lips like blood, then slow sly smiles of passion towards me. "I give up!" I yelled to them, "take me, break me, just let me have a taste."

Did I say that out loud? Here at Kenny's? Get a grip, man. It's been months without pasta, weeks without even a kiss on the lips, don't dwell on it, concentrate on standing, get money from my pocket, order something, breathe deeply. My eyes wandered below.

Apple pie. There was apple pie, apple goddamn pie! Under heat lamps of their own, triangles of flaking golden pleasure relaxed side by side, elegant ladies having a chat. They called out for me to join them, "Come on in, honey. Don't you want to come in and play?" I answered them immediately and most definitely out loud, "I'll be right there!" I rubbed my hand down my face like a drunk, I felt the back of my neck, I was dripping sweat while I stared at the lovely apple pies and words came out of my mouth without my command, I whispered to them, "I love you." My eyelids fell slowly, I was going to pass out.

"Hey mistah," voices came from somewhere else and I looked over to the bubbling brown broth of barbeque sauce and rising slowly out was a set of stunning baby back ribs. They rose up and twisted and curved and came to life in front of my own eyes. The sticky sauce dripped from her so slowly that even time stopped to watch. She was thick and dark and juicy and tangy and wanted me, needed my fingers to rub in the sauce, to massage her, to feel her. I needed her right now, in my mouth, on my tongue, dripping from my lips. She opened her mouth, "Hey mistah," she said with a wink, a breathless, dreamy voice. "Did you miss me?" Oh yeah I did. Oh yes I did, yes I do! I do! I do! "I'll be good to you!" I said, maybe out loud again, oh who cares. Tears formed in my eyes.

I started to understand the hyenas in Tanzania, their thirst for blood, their heightened concentration, their lust for flesh. I was an animal, a focused, hungry animal with only one thing on its mind. Well, maybe a few things.

More voices bounced through the air and I looked around and quickly found them. Lined up next to each other, posing under the hot spotlights, golden chicken glistened in oil and juices: legs, wings, thighs, breasts. Poultry supermodels, tanning blond goddesses soaking up the warm rays of sun, chatting casually with the ears of golden corn, whispering noncha- lantly to the sauces. Playing hard to get. But one particular juicy blonde was eyeing me like a hooker on a street corner. She was plump and luscious, her skin was oily and lightly tanned, wet and glistening, I could almost taste the salty sweat of her thighs. I swallowed. I was two bus stops past delirium. I watched her roll around in her oil bath and I didn't know whether to hug her, kiss her, eat her, or take her to the chapel and marry her, but we were going to have a long-term, meaningful relationship. She was speaking directly to me now, but I couldn't hear it right, it worried me deeply that it was a dream, I went in closer. A soft, low roar of a voice, a '50s pin-up girl, a deep whisper, the entire Southeast Asian continent went silent so that I could hear what she was going to say, one word that I had to lean over to hear: "Hungry?"

I stopped breathing.

In the distance, I started to hear more and more voices, I couldn't make them out, but they kept repeating. I looked up and saw Saint Peter at the gates of heaven, reincarnated as a Malaysian teenager dressed in a Kenny Rogers uniform with a nametag that said "Koh." He was looking in my direction and finally the words sank in, "Mistah? Hey mistah!" he said over and over, I don't want to know since when, but he was real. "Hey mistah, you OK? You going to eat now, mistah?"

Bradley Charbonneau now lives extremely close to several juicy restaurants in San Francisco. He writes about love, travel, and the love of travel. You can see more of his work at www.bradleycharbonneau.com.

* * *

Life in the Oncoming Lane

Adventures in public transit in Paraguay.

YOU'RE WAITING ON THE CORNER OF EUSEBIO AYALA AND San Martin, or is it Avenida Argentina and General Diaz? Who can keep it all straight when street names change on any given corner? Anyway, somebody told you to wait by the horse statue to catch a bus out of Asunción, and you're anxious to get out of the carbon monoxide-filled streets of the capital. You've seen several buses that would help you to accomplish this goal, but all of them fly right by despite your frantic hand-waving. It's odd how others stand patiently with one arm outstretched, calmly hailing their buses. You'll have to try this *tranquilo* approach next time.

Several unfamiliar lines pass, one splattering you with greasy muck. You're having a hard time seeing the numbers on the buses. You try the subtle approach, and the bus slows enough for you to hop on.

¡Que cool! *"¿Esto pasa por San Bernadino?"*

"¿Qué?"

"¿San Ber?"

"No."

Oh man! The bus is picking up speed as you dive out the door. A kind lady tells you that you're on the wrong side of the street. Oops!

Your luck seems to be changing! Just as you cross, an appropriate bus is arriving. Too bad you're not at a marked bus stop. It honks and darts past. You rush down to the official stop. Here comes a sure thing. This line is guaranteed to take you where you want to go. It's a popular line, and you get kicked, shoved, stepped on, and elbowed. As you politely back off to allow a pregnant woman to board, three people slip into the gap. An old woman shoves you backwards. The bus begins to move. You, the overly courteous North American, manage to get one foot on board.

It's not quite as easy to hang on and duck signs and telephone poles as you thought. One particularly hazardous turn sends the guy in the back door onto the curb. The *chofer* seems to believe that, since that guy "got off," there's room for more. He cuts off a defenseless and helmetless motorcyclist to pick up a crowd of passengers. Guess what? There is room! You get crushed into the bus.

Face to the windshield, you realize your life is in the hands of a lunatic. The *chofer* is steering with his elbows while counting his money. You hand him a 5,000 guarani bill. Bad move! He hands you back 3,000. You know the fare is only 1,000 and ask for the correct change. The *chofer* goes back to licking his fingers and flipping through his bills. You begin to argue, but as the *chofer* divides his attention between the wad of bills and his "what-you-gonna-do-'bout-it" look (did you really think driving got even a fraction?), a head-on collision with a petrol truck is narrowly avoided. You decide to let it slide and push your way to a spot *un poco más por atrás*, saying, *"perdon, permiso, disculpe…"* with each shove, bump, and kick. People are staring. You shut up and stay put, your pelvis wedged between a seat back and a giant sack of manioc. You imagine how embarrassing it would be to get medevaced because you fractured your tush on a Third World bus.

While you stand there with the tingling sensation of your hands losing circulation, you try to ignore the stares of other passengers. Remember…it's just because you're a gringa, not because you have an enormous zit, horrendous body odor, or a crusty city-soot booger sprouting from one nostril. Just in case, you check your face in the *soldadito's* cool reflective shades (Oh boy! Did you just make eye contact?!), do a subtle pit check, and poke a pinky up each nostril.

All right! A seat nearby opens up! You push the nine-year-old beer salesman out of the way and grab it! You try to relax, but this voice in your head keeps repeating: "Please remain seated. Keep your hands and all items inside the bus at all times. This *linea* is not responsible for lost, stolen, or damaged property. At the sound of the buzzer, push forward on the safety bar and pull back. The Cordillera de los Altos will be reaching speeds of ninety kilometers per hour with frequent screeching halts. So hold on! We hope you enjoy your time at Six Flags over Paraguay!"

You have a lovely window seat. Too bad the window is stuck shut and the guy in front of you is smoking. The eighty-year-old hombre, who wouldn't move in for you to sit, is hitting on you in Guarani. You only remember the *grose-rias* you learned in training, so you nod and smile. He's groping himself. Now he's reaching to grope you. You suddenly remember the great advice of a veteran volunteer: You point to his groin and begin to snicker, gradually working up to some hysterical, rib-clutching, eye-watering, gut-busting laughter. The poor guy is so embarrassed he flees and gets off the bus.

You need to get off shortly, so you move to the aisle side and allow three kids into the window seat. Across the aisle are an adorable little boy and a girl with a chicken in her lap. Wouldn't that make a precious photo? You ask to take their picture. *"¡Si!"* This'll be a great one to send home. You feel just like Kathleen Turner in *Romancing the Stone*. Just as you shoot this potential National Geographic photo, the adorable little boy tosses his cookies…and *empanadas*…and whatever else he consumed in the last twelve hours.

WHOOPS! A *chipera* with swinging hips and a lethal basket of chipa just booted your camera out of your hand! I guess, since the *puertita* popped open, that not only is your award-winning photo ruined, but probably also the ones of your unapproved trip to Iguaçu Falls. Well, you can always go back to Brazil.

You watch anxiously for your stop. Your friend told you to get off by the Despensa Familia—that should be easy to find. You spot it almost immediately and hit the buzzer. Ten blocks and two buzzes later, the *chofer* slows down enough for you to jump off. You walk back the ten blocks to the *despensa* to find that the Despensa Familia you were looking for is fifteen kilometers down the road. You'll want to take a bus to get back there.

You're back in the capital after a fairly *tranquilo* ride from the *campo*. Your leg is asleep since some lady plopped her kid into your lap for safekeeping the entire trip; and your neck is a little cramped from balancing someone's handbag on your head.

As you walk towards Calle Última you realize your rear end has fallen asleep. You wish your bladder would do the same. You hop on the first Linea 15 that you encounter, realizing that this is the 15 that runs down all the cobblestone streets on its run to the Peace Corps office.

After a long day in the office, avoiding your APCD (Assistant Peace Corps Director) and watching the latest batch of *Seinfeld* videos, you head back to a friend's site for the night. You take a Linea 31 to the horse statue and wait for this great bus that will take you right past her corner. It comes only every half-hour, but what are the chances that you just missed one?

You count buses to pass the time. You count to 100. It's been over a half-hour. *Tranquilo, no más.* You decide to take the next bus heading to her town, no matter what line. You count to 50. All the buses are packed with people hanging out the doors. You flag down the next one anyway.

You once again find yourself hanging out the door. You have great bus surfing skills, but you need two feet on the floor to do it. Luckily, there's a very nice guy standing in the door with you, holding you in with one arm. You start to feel attracted to him.

Your brief, but intimate, relationship ends abruptly as you get shoved up a step. You find yourself in the arms of yet another attractive Paraguayan man. In fact, this whole trip proves to be a long sequence of brief intimate encounters. However, you are now a veteran volunteer and are very *tranquila*.

You finally get a seat just as you get into town. Unfortunately, it's the seat over the wheel and, when you put your feet on the hump, all your tediously collected bus change falls onto the floor…behind you. Well, you need to keep your eyes on the road for your stop, so you just let it go. But you realize that you've never had a seat on this particular route, and you don't recognize anything. You search the shoulder for familiar potholes.

You make your way to the back of the bus and pull the cord. The bus turns and speeds up. You pull again. The bus turns and speeds up...again! You pull again. The bus turns and slows down. You hop off and sprain your ankle. You wonder if you can take a side trip to the office tomorrow and get per diem for this?

You are lost. It's starting to rain. Your foot hurts. And there's something else that just isn't quite right. You suddenly realize...your bra is gone!

Kendra Lachniet is an English and Spanish teacher in Hillman, Michigan. She served in the Peace Corps from 1992 to 1994 in the town of Coronel Bogado in Paraguay. She still enjoys traveling despite her numerous misadventures, most of them involving public transportation.

* * *

Sleepless in Florence

It's not his bride who's keeping him up.

DORMIRE. THAT'S THE ITALIAN VERB MEANING "TO SLEEP." Sounds very melodic, smooth, soothing, doesn't it? Say it again to yourself, if you want. Very slowly, pronouncing every syllable, rolling your tongue on the "r" if you're feeling exotic.

But while *dormire* is a lovely word, and very fun to say, it's also a highly ironic member of the Italian language. Because while it's clearly right there on page 53 of *Webster's English-Italian Dictionary*—sandwiched between *dormiglione* ("sleepy head") and *dormitorio* ("dormitory")—the concept of sleep, as we quickly discover, apparently does not exist in real, everyday Italian life. Not for us, anyway. Not at 3 Tavolini in Florence.

It has been a week or so since we moved into our new apartment. It's great to have a "home base," a place we'll be able to call our own for the next few months. 3 Tavolini is spacious, central to everything, couldn't be more convenient. But one problem: it's loud. No, it's beyond loud. It's loud on steroids. Celia and I could have spent the past ten years in the West Bank, downtown Mogadishu—any place where artillery shells explode on a regular basis—and this would *still* be the loudest place we've ever lived. Loretta, the landlady, conveniently forgot to mention that at six each morning, a construction crew arrives next door. Their workday consists of yelling, throwing ceramic tiles at each other, and smashing our wall with blunt instruments. All while listening to that maddening Kylie Minogue "Na Na Na" song on the repeat setting, at full volume, for eight straight hours.

Fine times here at 3 Tavolini, fine times indeed. But the daytime noise isn't the real problem; it's the after-hours noise. This place is loud even at 3:46—wait, make that 3:47—in the morning. I've tried counting sheep, stuffing my ears with cotton, having Celia shoot me with the alcoholic equivalent of elephant tranquilizers, but nothing gets me to sleep. The streets outside are still very much alive in the wee hours, and from the sounds of it, don't seem to be dying down anytime soon. That's why right now, instead of sleeping, I'm sitting at our kitchen table and writing about *not* sleeping. Anything to avoid lying wide awake in my bed listening to the yelling, babbling, idiot-drunk tourists *still* stumbling home from the bars and clubs. (The accordion player at the outdoor restaurant right under our window sure isn't doing me any favors either. I think he's on his twelfth encore.) I don't know where I'm going with this. Being fresh out of sheep (and elephant tranquilizers), I'm honestly just killing time here.

Celia says that I can never sleep when I have something serious on my mind, when I'm stressed. Like in the weeks leading up to when I proposed. Unbeknownst to her, I was in the process of buying her ring, emptying a significant chunk of my savings, worrying about how it would all go, all that pre-engagement stuff. Not that I was worried about whether she'd say yes (I don't know how men can ask women to marry them without being at least 75 percent sure they'll say yes). But I was just all worked up about whether the engagement would happen the way she'd always wanted. Whether it would be romantic enough. Whether I'd remember the ring. Whether I'd pass out or not. In those two weeks leading up to our engagement trip to Germany I think I slept a total of ten hours.

But trust me, stress has not been the cause of my sleepless nights here in Florence. I haven't had anything truly stressful within a six-mile radius of my mind since we quit our jobs and came here. Yes, there's been some culture shock while getting settled and some petty little arguments between Celia and me. But, as with anything, it's all relative. Compared to job stress, family stress, Mass Pike commuter stress, deadline stress, salary stress, bill-paying stress—in short, the American stress we faced every day of our lives back home—Florence stress barely registers on the Richter scale, especially now that we're out of the Chateau d' Mosquito Bite and have found an affordable apartment right in the center of the city. And while 3 Tavolini is no paradise, it's a place to call "home" for at least the next three months, so an Atlas-like weight has been lifted off our shoulders. As a result, the most stressful issues I now have to face each day are when to get out of bed, whether to go running, what to have for lunch and dinner, and whether we'll go to Lake Como, Capri, or Cinque Terre for our first big trip. I'm not exactly tackling quantum physics or solving world hunger here.

And now that Celia has signed up for an Italian class and is in school four hours every day (nine A.M. until one P.M.), I have plenty of quiet, peaceful "Mark time" to write. In short, life is good. Therefore, tonight and every night I should be able to *dormire* like a *bambino*, right? No. Not right. Not right at all. Not in Florence, or, as I've come to call it—The City of Really Loud Things and Annoying People Who Keep You Awake All Night. For starters, there's our upstairs neighbor.

We've never laid eyes on her. But trust me, she's there. (I just heard her a few minutes ago, in fact). She was away for our first couple of days here, based on the large pile of mail just inside the front door downstairs. But the last few nights she's returned with a stomping, furniture-moving vengeance. All Loretta told us was that she's "a Japanese gal," but unless she's also a sumo wrestler, I have a hard time understanding how she can make the monumental racket that she does. The Japanese women I've had living above me during my lifetime have always been quiet, dignified, polite little beings. Granted, there have only been two—Babson College exchange students named Satomi and Pachanci who were from Nagasaki and rented our attic bedroom when I was about ten. They would shamefully excuse themselves if they so much as *thought* too loudly.

Our Japanese friend here, on the other hand, is not only loud, she's apparently an avid clog dancer, which is a nice cross-cultural touch. She's clearly failed to grasp the concept of walking around in her socks, because the constant, echoing *clackety-slam-clack-slam-SLAM!* of her 95-pound shoes practically tears the enamel off your teeth. Eleven P.M., two A.M., ten minutes ago. It doesn't matter what time it is. When she has an urge to practice the latest steps, she straps on the clogs and "cuts loose, footloose, kick off your Sunday shoes." During some of my more serious insomniac trances I've actually considered how much it would cost to import African termites and set them loose in the building. They might destroy everything within a four-block radius, including our own belongings, but if they devoured those goddamn wooden shoes in the process it'd be worth it.

Then there's her furniture. For some reason I can't even begin to explain without a team of psychiatrists and several bottles of whiskey, our friend upstairs feels that this ungodly time of night is absolutely ideal to move her furniture. Usually anywhere between eleven P.M. and four A.M., our ceiling suddenly explodes into action with sounds worthy of little Batman cartoon exclamation balloons: *Stomp! Bang! Crash! Blam! Klorg! Crack! Womp!* Immediately awake despite the cotton balls that Celia and I have started jamming into our ears, I lie there and listen to her drag her couches, chairs, end tables, and floor lamps all over her clearly uncarpeted apartment. Not to mention her fireplace irons, golf clubs, tin pots and pans, humidifier and dehumidifier, skis, boots and poles, bagpipes, suit of armor, and twelve-piece steel drum kit—while wearing her heavy wooden clogs, instead of, say, some soft bunny slippers.

Just as I'm convinced that all of her belongings are on the verge of crashing through our ceiling and that of the apartment below us, she stops for a brief moment. Silence. Sweet, sweet silence. Usually a minute, maybe two if she's feeling magnanimous. While slowly drifting back to sleep, I figure she's paused briefly to either: a) gauge the positive energy flow created by her new living-room design concept or; b) greedily inhale another ten lines of uncut Bolivian marching powder in order to reenergize and start batting her 300-pound Louis XIV armoire around. It's probably the coke, because no human can have this much energy without the aid of a controlled substance. Unless it's not a Japanese woman at all, but, rather, her pet monkey who, while his owner is away, gets into the saki, sniffs glue, and rides a three-wheel ATV around the apartment while blowing into a kazoo and smashing giant marching band cymbals together.

And did I mention the karaoke machine? Yes, there's more fun going on upstairs than just a Dutch two-step. She doesn't unleash karaoke on us every night, mind you, like her mobile furniture and extensive wooden footwear collection. But when she does decide that she's lost that lovin' feelin, it's raining men, or that she will, indeed, survive, you know it immediately. You hear her dragging a heavy object across her floor, followed by what sounds like a few rubberized microphones and power cords dragging behind it. I've played in bands, so I know what amps, mixing boards, and power cords sound like when dragged across a stage. And that's just what our ceiling becomes: a stage. *Ladies and gentlemen, welcome to Amateur Karaoke Night in lovely Florence, Italy!*

What comes next I can only describe as two alley cats shagging on trash cans. Sporadically, and not the least bit rhythmically, her off-key wailing and ghastly screeching permeates our ceiling along with a pre-fab, pulsating drum-and-bass disco club beat. She makes Yoko Ono sound like Maria Callas. We practically fall out of bed and start flopping in pain on the cold, tile floor, covering our ears, shaking our heads, "NO! NO! NO! NO!" our mouths agape and eyes bulging, like in some cheesy sci-fi movie when the aliens aim their supersonic brain-melter ray guns at the helpless humans who cower and squirm in the streets below. Thank God there are no dogs in the neighborhood, or little canine heads would be exploding at an alarming rate. Thankfully, again, it isn't every night that our neighbor decides to entertain us with her musical stylings, but even twice a week is enough. It stays with you, in the back of your mind, like something terrible that happened to you in your childhood and occasionally frightens you awake in the dark, sweating and panting, praying it'll just go away once and for all and

you can find your happy place again, find your happy place,
happy place...

*Mark St. Amant is a humor writer whose day job is writing advertis-
ing copy for national clients such as McDonald's, the U.S. Marine
Corps, and Volkswagen. He also plays acoustic guitar in local bars
in Boston, and is the founder/editor/writer of "The Sports Rag,"
a satire sports web site that has been hailed by ESPN radio as
"hilarious." This story was excerpted from his as-yet-unpublished
book,* The Running of the Boar: Travel Tales and Other Random
Musings About One Newlywed Couple's Move to Italy.

LARRY HABEGGER

* * *

The Curse of Monolingualism

*An embarrassed American finds himself at
sea in a French-speaking copy shop.*

I NEVER FEEL ILL AT EASE IN A COUNTRY WHERE I DON'T
speak the language. Whether it's Tibetan or Swahili, Tagalog
or Sinhala, I just smile, act out, try some sign language, and
make friends. But French, French is a different story. When
faced with French, I flee in terror. All of the languages I have
ever studied crowd my brain and I can't find my bearings. My
failure with French always makes me feel that I have failed as
a human being. Is it not the language of the civilized world?
Or have the French just convinced us that this is so?

I needed to make eighty-five copies of a simple two-page
handout for a workshop I was leading at the Geneva Writers'
Conference. When I entered a big camera store that I was
told had copy machines, I followed signs around to the back
for "photocopies," a good English word in this French-speaking international Swiss city.

I was still jet-lagged from my long trip from San Francisco
so I wasn't thinking clearly, but I knew how this errand
would go at home: I'd find the machine, get a counter car-

tridge, set the controls for eighty-five copies stapled in the upper left corner, hit the start button, pick up my copies, and pay. I'd be in and out in five minutes tops.

The young man behind the counter looked blankly at me when I asked in English if I could use the machine. I tried again and he replied in French. I blushed with embarrassment, feeling foolish, understanding nothing. I showed him the sheets I wanted to copy, pointed to the machine, and tried to make him understand that I wanted to use it. He came and stood next to me, as uncertain of how to proceed as I was. I began to shuffle from one foot to the other, heat rising on my cheeks, hair prickling on my neck. I stood there mute, trying to think of a way to communicate what I wanted. How do the French do this? Why did I not remember anything beyond the most rudimentary French words? Was I not an educated individual? No, I was no better than your everyday monolingual American buffoon turned loose in a bastion of European refinement.

He seemed to understand that I wanted to use the machine, and by gesturing at my document I conveyed that I needed my copies stapled. His face lit up and he scurried behind the counter, emerging with a stapler. I had been trying to ask if the machine could do this, but never mind, it was progress. I couldn't determine what the cost of copying would be. Two signs on the wall suggested two prices, the lowest of which appeared to be ten centimes. But how would I keep track of the number of copies?

More babbling in English and replies in French, many gestures this way and that, and suddenly I understood. Of course, it's coin operated! I pulled out a bill, offered it to him, and uttered, shamelessly, "Change," trying to make it sound French ("shaange"). He shook his head and pointed around the corner to the cash registers.

No one there spoke English either, but my dog-like utterances of "Shaange, *gracias*, I mean, *si'l vous plait*, shaange, shaange, *si'l vous plait danke*," got my point across, and moments later I had four five-franc coins in hand. (I learned later that I'd had it all wrong—the word for "change" in French is *monnaie*.) Back at the machine, I fed in money, got the job started, and stood back to watch the sheets spitting out.

When they were finished I repeated the process with my second sheet, then began stapling at another counter. A few copies into the job the machine stopped. I turned just as the clerk hurried around the counter. We got to the machine at the same time, and I pointed to the paper tray saying it must be out of paper, because I thought I had put in plenty of money. He pointed to the coin box and muttered something, then lifted the cover, moved my sheet out of the way, put down a receipt he needed to copy, stuck a key in the coin box to activate the machine, then hit the start button just as I was blurting "Stop! Stop! I'll lose track of my count—" when he too realized his mistake as the machine began running off sixty copies of his receipt—"*Merde!*" he barked and slammed something to make it stop.

Embarrassed, he took his copies and gave me an apologetic look. I fed more money into the machine, hoping for the best. Later it stopped again, hungry for more money, and I dropped in my last coin (twenty francs now!). Eventually it spit out the last copy.

Relieved, I pushed a button on the coin box to get my change but nothing came out. As I stood there contemplating one final foray into monolingual debasement, the clerk appeared at my side. So I tried to explain, now feeling ridiculous, with gestures and worthless English, that I needed to get my unspent money back. He opened the paper tray to see if this time the machine was indeed out of paper.

"No, I'm finished, *finis*," I said, trying to pronounce the word correctly, pointing to the coin box showing money left over. A look of comprehension passed over his face and he said, "One moment," (English!) and went to get someone.

I resumed stapling, then he came back with a woman, explaining in French, and she unlocked the coin box, then disappeared. Minutes later she returned, spoke to me in French holding out some coins, and I stammered yet again that I didn't speak French. "Oh!" she gasped, her hand covering her mouth. She spoke to another woman across the room, who looked up, said "*Oui*," and the woman handed me the coins with a relieved smile.

I didn't know what to do except pocket the money, say "*merci beaucoup*" and really mean it, even though "*gracias*" almost shouldered it aside in my addled brain. I finished my stapling, packed up and looked around for the clerk to thank him for enduring this ordeal with me, but he had vanished, perhaps to avoid any further "conversation" with the American buffoon.

On the way out it occurred to me, though, with the sudden clarity of all fresh thoughts, that I wasn't the only monolinguist in the shop. As far as English was concerned, everyone I spoke to was a monolinguist, and even though I admit it was a sorry excuse for me to cling to, the thought gave me a certain comfort. I shouldn't have beaten myself up so much. In dealing with me they were as impaired as I was dealing with them. They were functionally monolingual, and I was a stranger in their midst. (Well, of course, they probably spoke German, Italian, Dutch, Danish, and ten other languages, but that was beside the point.)

Partway back to the hotel I pulled the coins from my pocket to see how much they'd given me. I was surprised to find fifteen francs. Even at the lowest posted price my 170 copies should have cost seventeen francs, so I got almost all of my money back! Sensing the karmic correctness of this result, I knew what I had to do. No, not return and embarrass myself further trying to explain their error. I would listen, without fear, to my French language tapes when I got home.

Larry Habegger is executive editor of the Travelers' Tales series. He is also coauthor of "World Travel Watch," a weekly syndicated column that appears in newspapers throughout the United States, on WorldTravelWatch.com, and on TravelersTales.com. He regularly teaches the craft of travel writing at workshops and writer's conferences, and is a popular writing coach (information at www.larryhabegger.com).

* * *

Egypt, Day One

What would you like to be accused of?

THE MAN LEANED DOWN, COUGHED, CLEARED HIS THROAT with a rough scraping sound and spat a massive, grayish brown glob of phlegm right in the center of my passport. "Isra-eli people shit!" he shouted. That was Mohammed Abdel. He ran the drink and food stand on the Egyptian-Israeli border near Taba.

"But I'm not an Israeli!" I pleaded softly and swallowed hard. "I didn't do anything!" I was just me. Innocent. I just came here.

"You go Isra-el." That was clear. It was the Israeli customs stamp from Ben Gurion Airport he spat on. "That already something. Isra-el shit." He dropped my passport in the dust and stomped on it several times then gave it a good kick. I stood in silence and watched. Was I supposed to be mad? Scared? Was this funny? Guido thought it was funny. Yes, Guido. A Swiss Guido.

"Why are you laughing *now*?" He had been laughing since I first met him.

"You are such an American," he said. "I have never met anybody quite like you."

"Then how do you know I am 'such an American'?" I growled at him. "I didn't do anything!"

"I know. That's so endearingly American as well. *I didn't do anything.*" He imitated me and began laughing again.

"What you like to drink?" Mohammed interrupted, his lung-oyster tirade complete. He swirled his full body robe behind the plywood and aluminium bar out of the sun and wind and laid on a huge smile. His over-sized mouth bunched up around his eyes and his moustache disappeared into his nose. It was a genuine smile. He even batted his eyelashes.

There were no taxis from the border that day. They were on strike and I was stuck with these guys. It was mid-January and there was not another tourist or traveler in sight, just a fat, lazy camel, strings of empty hotels in the distance, and a small, filthy girl with blue eyes who brought drinks and food to the stand from somewhere out in the sand. Every time she passed, she asked me for money. Each time I said no, she told me to "fuck off." She was not more than seven years old and I found her rather mysterious.

The buses were working though. A bus was indeed coming, but it wouldn't arrive until seven in the evening. It was not quite eight A.M. when I crossed the border. "Fanta?" I answered and Guido laughed again.

Guido was with me at the border. At customs I showed the young guard that you could eat vitamin C. He wasn't any older than me, and until that moment had been all smiles. When I put the pill in my mouth and chewed it he backed away as if I were a ghost. From behind the bench he jerked a thick wooden truncheon and crashed it into the bottle in my hand. It splintered and tiny round pills filled the air. My knees trembled as he began screaming to his superiors as if he were a child and I a madman throttling his dearest teddy bear. His eyes were hollow, full of fright. I could only think: *Midnight Express* comes true.

Soldiers, police, and customs agents. The tiny cement and plywood shack that served as customs and passport check filled with men, pistols, automatic rifles, flying sticks, badges, and moustaches. One rough-looking officer jerked my bag from the customs table and dumped its entire contents into the dust and began kicking them around. Another pointed some kind of rifle at me.

"Hey!" It was a feeble protest but I was frozen. "I didn't do anything!" Behind me, a tall, lanky European guy cracked up. He was the only other person crossing the border with me. "What's so funny!?! What's so fucking funny!"

"They are tearing apart your baggage," he answered and kept on with a full belly laugh.

"That's not funny! Goddammit!" But clearly I was wrong. By now, everyone seemed to be laughing. Suddenly there were no more guns, no truncheons, and everyone was looking down and picking through my gear.

"What!?!" I yelled at the Egyptians.

"You have so many things! Why you bring so many things?" They were poking through my possessions now with curiosity. "What this?"

"First aid kit."

"What this?"

"Extra underwear. My mom said…"

"You are panties smuggler?" the roughest looking officer asked, and they all laughed.

"What this?"

"Shit." Actually, that was funny. It was a two-way breathing mask for mouth-to-mouth resuscitation; the gift of a paranoid mother. The plastic tube allowed you to blow air into the injured person without actually touching them. "Nothing."

"What this?

"More vitamins." I had enough of these to choke the Budweiser Clydesdale Team. At this they got serious.

"No, no, no…" Then the men proceeded to gather up all my vitamins, including the individual vitamin C tablets that were scattered all over the room, empty each bottle into a huge, clear plastic bag and take them away. There was chattering in Arabic and more laughing from the back room and it somehow felt good to know that I was the source of someone's amusement. The young border guard who had initially screamed, gathered all my things into a neat pile, folded my clothes and proceeded to very politely reload my bag.

"They will talk about you for years," said the European. I gave him a seriously dirty look, grabbed my bag and walked away.

In the afternoon, Mohammed, Guido, and I sat out in the brain-searing sun admiring the camel against the backdrop of cement and glass hotels. It was round and fat and slow. It seemed quite a healthy animal and we talked about it for a long time. The girl had spat at me on the last pass and missed. Mohammed insisted she was flirting with me. "Right," I said.

"A game of chess?" Guido offered. He had stopped laughing with the heat. "I hate the heat," he told us. Mohammed said the only cure for the heat was coffee and so after our fifth or sixth Fanta, and a couple of hours of animated discussion about Israel's right to exist and a fat camel, we began drinking coffee. By then it was afternoon. Wasn't there any water around here? "Yes, sure, sure," Mohammed announced and pointed out at the Gulf of Aqaba. Then he burst into laughter. Guido joined him. I wanted water.

We dragged a flimsy card table out in the dust and fixed an old red parasol next to it for shade. Decades of cars, and centuries of feet and hooves had trampled the ground around us to a fine powder. There was not a single piece of vegetation within 100 yards and every short breath of putrid, chrome-melting air blowing out of the Sinai added another layer of dust to us. If we hadn't moved, we would have been completely covered in a matter of days.

Guido was quick to beat both of us in chess. Slaughtering us actually, in a matter of minutes. Mohammed and I spent the next several hours in competition, each trying painfully not to gain the title of "the worst chess player in Taba." Then we all sat in silence and watched the camel. It didn't move. It just stared back at us. The little girl came again. "Fuck you," she said. She wasn't carrying anything anymore and not asking for money. She existed just to insult me and I began to feel a bit intimidated by her. Then we decided to drink beer.

"The problem is," Guido began suddenly after we had polished off a few rounds. "You Americans think that you are individuals. In fact, you are *not* and that is why you cannot understand that someone might hate you for being an American."

"But I am not my government," I protested. It was the most intelligent thing I could get out of my contracting, water-starved brain.

"But you support American government," Mohammed joined in. "You support American government and American businessmen and you buy what is stolen from other countries." He sat back triumphantly, having made his point.

"I just live my life."

"And you just living your life deeply affects people in other parts of the world and you don't realize that. You cannot even comprehend such things. So, you get attacked and think *but I didn't do anything—why do they hate me?*" Guido was clear.

"It is because of what you do do," Mohammed said firmly.

"My gut is going to fall out if I don't get water in my body. I need some water." I changed the subject and again we fell to silence, watching the camel as if it were a television. My eyes crossed, my head hurt, and then I passed out.

Just after six o'clock a beaten-up bus flew through the dust, squealing to a halt just inches from our table. I lurched onto the ground. There was yelling, bumping, and scurrying about. The table fell over and the parasol blew under the bus and snapped with a bang. Then Guido was gone. So was the bus. It dragged the parasol a couple dozen yards and then spat it out. It lay, spinning slowly in the road.

"You pay me."

"What?"

"You pay me…." I can't recall what Mohammed demanded but I gave him a pocket full of Israeli shekels and a few Egyptian pounds. He seemed satisfied and disappeared into the shade of the hutch. I looked around. Shit.

"Was that the bus?"

"That was the bus."

Shit. "When is the next one?"

There was no answer. I pulled myself out of the dust and held my head. I had my first and worst sugar-caffeine-alcohol hangover of my life and it was killing me. I staggered around for a few minutes and tried to spit on the camel.

Eventually, I gathered my passport from the dust, slung my bag over my shoulder, and threw Mohammed a few extra pounds. He said nothing, sitting silently as if a sage, staring deeply into the reflection of the sunset glaring from one of the hotels.

I walked south along the coast road for the next three days, living on the water the taxi drivers brought me.

Jim O'Donnell holds a Master's Degree in Community and Regional Planning from the University of New Mexico. He has spent too many years wandering the Earth, while his gardens wilted at home. He married a tri-lingual Finn in 2001 and they are expecting their first child. Jim's writings have appeared in Call of the Wild, Catch?, *and* Conceptions Southwest, *as well as the Finnish nature magazine* Suomen Luonto (Finnish Nature). *He is currently working on a book about his recent 1,500-mile walk across Finland.*

JULIETTE KELLEY

Kayaking for Weenies

What did you do on your summer vacation?

AS A RULE, I AM NOT MUCH ON TROPICAL VACATIONS BECAUSE they mean sunburn, insects that fly (and subsequently bite), and worst of all, squeezing into a bathing suit. So it was against all my natural tendencies to fly off to Maui with my two thin, tanned, cute friends. This was particularly true for me, nearing fifty, out of shape, and hovering close to two hundred pounds. Some people who love you will tell you to stay by the pool, drinking a compelling assortment of tropical refreshments: hula girls, blue moons, mai tais, and chi chis (unlike the mainland, this is not a euphemism for breasts). They will encourage you to catch up on your reading and saturate yourself with SPF Number 50 suntan oil. My traveling companions did not give me this advice. Instead, they encouraged me to challenge myself with new and different experiences involving danger and possible death. I proudly survived the helicopter ride. Then I managed the snorkeling mere steps from the hotel beach. So, when I again blindly followed my favorite women in the entire world—who were already resourceful, fit, and funny—on a four-hour sea kayaking trip to "swim with dolphins," I was inoculated with a heavy dose of false optimism.

There were warning signs about this trip, but we ignored them. For example, we were required to be downstairs in the hotel lobby by 6:15 A.M. so that a local boy (described by his boss as "cranky") could pick us up. This description alone should have been a clue to what the day might hold. However, Local Boy was not cranky, just late and catatonic. Even with his tardiness, his eerie silence, and the really bad shocks on what amounted to a recycled "band bus," we arrived at the designated place in plenty of time to begin our adventure. At the staging area, a clot of white tourists stood around dazed, while Dolph, the sadomasochistic company owner, barked angry orders to us in a thick Germanic accent.

Our fellow travelers tried on equipment, afraid to mention if something didn't fit. The life jackets smelled vaguely of mildewed fear, the kind you expect to feel on death-trap roller coasters. Again, a possible forewarning, but naturally we all ignored it.

Ocean kayaking is not easy, in spite of what the brochures tell you. According to travel-book blurbs and hotel magazines, you can jump into a kayak and paddle to Japan by lunch, frolicking with dolphins and sea turtles on the way. For overweight weenies like me, it is not so simple. First there are the waves—big-ass waves, huge waves. Shoving off was an unfortunate time to remember that people come from all over the world to surf in the big waves in Maui. This was not New Jersey.

Then there are the kayaks, these teeny, tiny fiberglass death traps supposedly designed to keep upright while tsunamis break over them. For the quick and agile, there is a learning curve of about eight years. However, for hung-over tourists who show up, pay eighty dollars, and expect to see dolphins, there should be some sort of driver's training simulator to make sure we don't have the reaction time of a sloth. It's not like that however. For us, the instructions were condensed to a thirty-second *Reader's Digest*-style warning, which roughly read: "Keep paddling, don't fall out, and oh, yeah, don't forget to have fun."

The guides did their best imitation of Tony Robbins motivational speeches to encourage us and tell us how much fun we were going to have. Afterwards, they begged for tips because in their words, "we have families to support and we only make minimum wage." The warning signs continued to mount.

Since there were three in my party and there were only one- and two-person kayaks, I needed a partner. Karen and Darla paired up and I was assigned to Elena, a somewhat friendly resident of Silicon Valley who seemed knowledgeable and confident. I was relieved to learn that she had kayaked before. I was also relieved to see that she had what looked like powerful shoulder muscles. I heard it was easier to control the rudder, so I volunteered to sit in the back. Being bold, Elena asked for a kayak in front of the group so we could shove off first; however Dolph, the little kayak-Nazi refused. ("You will sit back here.") For me, it was a mixed blessing. Elena did not take to orders well. I saw jaw muscles clench.

After selecting our kayaks, slathering on tubes of sunscreen, getting into our gear, and suiting up in smelly life vests, we were shoved out into the ocean by the two cute tip-seeking Blond Boy Guides. The first seven minutes were a blast. Then I got tired. My arms started to ache and instead of heading out with the group, Elena and I were traveling in circles thanks to my impeccable ability to use my paddle as a rudder. Trying to help, Elena kept shouting to "paddle right" and then "paddle left" but somehow we still weren't going forward. She continued to bark makeshift instructions, which I honestly thought I was following, until Blond Boy Guide #2 came up and offered to give us a tow to the first stopping place. I was overjoyed, but I could tell Elena, a seasoned kayaker, was mortified.

I can't quite say I mastered the art of steering the kayak but Elena and I managed to stay up with the group (thanks to the tow) until we reached a cove aptly named "The Aquarium." The Blond Boy Guides dragged the kayaks up over the lava beds to find a comfortable place to put on our snorkel gear. Decked out appropriately, we trundled into the water.

I think Darla summed it up best when she popped up her sweet blond head and screamed, "It's like a damn aquarium down here!" The Blond Boy Guides "high-fived" each other while sharing a Kodak moment with an "it's all worth it" grin.

Below was truly an underwater wonderland. It was the oceanic version of Disneyland and Marine World and every other middle-class outing kids dream of taking. There were popsicle-colored tropical fish darting through seaweed and lava rock, spotted eels, and gooey looking corals. But it was the sea turtle that stole my heart. She was a baby just turtling around looking for treats with her big cow eyes. She let me follow her all over the cove, coming up for air and submerging again for another look around. With my snorkeling vest and zaftig body, I was probably the shape of her mama.

After lunch, during the second leg and the third hour of our "four-hour" kayak trip, things really went a little sideways. First, I'll admit I was already really tired. I had seen enough, and frankly, I was totally fucking done. I closed my eyes to visualize a mai tai and a cabana chair flanked by the requisite cute cabana boy. But the Blond Boy Guides had more fun in store for us.

We were off to a place called the "Fish Bowl" to see more fish. Elena and I headed off with the group. But it seemed that the three-sentence orientation on sea kayaking did not prepare us for the giant ocean swells that began to rock around us. It was during one of these bursting waves that we were knocked overboard. I didn't worry much about drowning. I had on a life jacket and everything on the kayak was strapped down. I *was* worried about hauling my body back into the kayak. Here is where going to the gym would have served me well. As it was, I did not have enough upper body strength to lift my big ass back up onto a kayak at sea to start out paddling again. I could tell by the look on Elena's face that she was one step away from swimming back to California. Blond Boy Guide #1 paddled up to our kayak and righted it with one hand. "O.K., girls, back up in the kayak," he shouted. With one smooth gesture, Elena heaved herself in and grabbed her paddle.

I, on the other hand, was not as agile. "I don't think I can do this." My voice was just a little tentative.

"Sure you can," Blond Boy Guide #1 assured me, "just lift yourself up and swing your legs in." He could have as easily been suggesting that I lift a Toyota; I wasn't "just lifting" anything.

Grunting, I hoisted myself up and up then slid back down. "Really, I can't do this by myself," I heaved. Blond Boy Guide #1 jumped out of his kayak and swam over to me.

"I will help you then. It is quite easy, just lift, then I will push you up." Again with the pig grunt, up and up. Boy Guide #1 slid his hand between my legs and like a skilled gynecologist pushed me up and propelled me, not into the boat but over the other side. "Oops. I pushed too hard, then." He was actually smiling. "One more time, this is it."

He came around to where I was bobbing like shark bait and we reassumed our positions. Again with the hand between my legs (this was turning out to be the most action I'd had in Hawai'i) I landed in the boat—for exactly thirty seconds before I managed to capsize the kayak, Elena, and me again.

Being a reasonable person without a death wish, Elena emerged from the water screaming "Get me out of her kayak! She doesn't know what she is doing!" I think that was a bit harsh, as I sort of knew what I was doing, I just didn't know how to get in the boat. Blond Boy Guide #2 relinquished his one-man kayak and Elena began to get the hell out of my way. Once again, but now with Blond Boy Guide #2 , we struggled to get me into the kayak with the "Perineal Assist." Again, over the side. It wasn't looking good, I was so exhausted and defeated, that I took the next logical step and began to cry. "I need a helicopter rescue," I implored.

"Those only happen in Jean Claude Van Damme movies. Out here, you have to keep paddling."

I looked out on the small gaggle of kayakers now gathered to watch me decompensate.

"No! I can't paddle, my lungs will explode. I know it. I have asthma, for God's sake. Send for a helicopter!"

I was pathetic now, crying and screaming to no avail. The thought crossed my mind that the guide just might be envisioning my death at sea.

"I'm gonna tow you in," said Blond Boy Guide #2. "It's real easy. This is something even you can do. Can you kick?"

"I guess." My bottom lip was quivering like a cocker spaniel's that has just peed on the rug.

"Great. Get to the back of the kayak and dog paddle like the kayak is a surfboard. I am going to tow you and the kayak into shore."

With a great deal of whining, I ended up doing as I was told. I am quite sure I looked like a beached elephant seal with goggles. The sea had calmed down, as it tends to do in the afternoon. We were now in the sixth hour of our four-hour kayak adventure. I don't know which was more humiliating—dog paddling to shore on the back end of a sea kayak or the applause I received from staff and fellow travelers. Missing on shore, of course, was Elena, who was probably calling her therapist.

Looking back, I probably should have suspected the worst when the hotel magazine offered a 50-percent-off coupon to use this particular company for our kayaking adventure. However, I can't say it wasn't a "unique and challenging experience." By the end of the day, I was sunburned and soggy. Out of the water, my legs were still trying to kick to shore while I undulated in invisible water.

After watching my ordeal from their own kayak, Karen and Darla considered it an achievement that we were all going back together, in one piece. We were also the last to get rides back to the hotel, so we ended up drinking local beer and smoking thick, round joints of Maui pot on the "band bus" with the Blond Boy Guides. Of course, this was not part of the advertised special but it was, by far, the most enjoyable part of the trip.

Juliette Kelley is a freelance writer in Northern California where she lives in her own Barbie Dream House with Ken and Skipper, her two male cats. Contrary to popular belief, she is not an athlete but she does keep her sanity by cycling through the Contra Costa County hills. She now stays alive by avoiding ocean sports.

JACQUELINE C. YAU

* * *

King Kong in Shanghai

If the cup fits, wear it.

I AM FIVE-FOOT, 4-INCHES AND 125 POUNDS. I HAVE A LONG, slim face, wide shoulders, long arms and legs, short-waist, skinny ankles, average-sized breasts, and a medium-sized butt. I'm about a size 8. I'm not your garden variety, extremely slim and petite Asian-American woman. O.K., hardly noteworthy in the United States but in China…I might as well be King Kong. I am HUGE. I am a deviant. I'm an alien squared because I actually resemble someone who belongs to the same race living in China but I'm shaped very differently. I find nothing fits me except for the occasional XXL.

I need a dress and I'm in China for another three months. I only brought functional wear, thinking that no one cares about fashion here. Silly me. I missed China's fast forward into consumerism in the four years since my last visit. I also surprise myself. I discover I want to look more feminine while I am in China. My good friend, Shirley, takes me to downtown Shanghai, to dressmaker row, to a *cheongsam* dressmaker she knows. The dresses stun the senses in copper, iridescent blue, bright green, searing red, sumptuous egg-plant—all luxuriant silk fabrics shot with gold threads and Asian patterns. I try to squeeze into a ready-made dress. Nope. Here in China, I'm a lush and voluptuous woman.

The dressmaker, a small fireball of a woman, charges over from the other side of the shop and takes over my dress selection, clucking and emitting a slew of Shanghainese and Mandarin phrases. She doesn't quite believe that I can't fit into any of the off-the-rack dresses. I look smaller than I am and taller than I am. My body is an optical illusion. People constantly misjudge my shape, size, weight, and age. She tries to stuff and zip me into a custom dress they are making for an Italian woman half my size. I think that Italian women and Chinese women must come from the same genetic stock judging from this dress—tiny people stock.

My Mandarin comprehension suffers a total breakdown when the excited shop staff surrounds me buzzing in two dialects, a deafening cacophony of sounds. The dressmaker summoned the entire staff out onto the shop floor to look at me. Two other girls from the back room, the dressmaker, the cashier, and now, a gathering horde of customers who just came in, gather to gawk at me, the human burrito. This is a society of people who stare. I am a sideshow. Passersby linger, looking in from the floor-to-ceiling picture windows behind me, no doubt wondering what is going on inside.

Hands touch me, prod me, poke me, as the dressmaker and her staff try to figure out why I can't fit into any of the dresses she has hanging on the racks. My body is a Tickle-Me Elmo toy to them. They confer. Finally, the dressmaker calms down enough to say in choppy English, "You have body of Eastern European woman. You need custom dress." They have never seen anything like this in a Chinese woman. I don't think that this is a compliment but they look in awe. I have visions of Soviet Bloc Olympians pumped full of steroids. That's me?

The dressmaker further states in a loud voice, "Your bra is no good…flimsy." I internally cringe. So now both my body and my underwear are under scrutiny. She measures me but tells me I will need to get re-measured after I come back wearing the correct bra. O.K. I can buy a new bra. No big deal. Lingerie has arrived in China. The dressmaker asserts that women are like flowers that need to be artfully arranged. I need structure, stiffness, and uplift to show off my lush Eastern European figure and their workmanship. I marvel at the sacrifices women make to look good, including myself, even in China.

As I walk from the dressmaker's shop, down a couple blocks to where the big department stores are, I notice that a full-scale war is in progress to persuade women that dressing pretty inside will make them feel great on the outside. Billboards lining the streets, on the sides of sleek new buildings, and all along the subway line, show beautiful glossy-haired Chinese women in skimpy lacy bra and underwear. Quite a change from the standard-issue shapeless silk or cotton waist-high briefs and undershirts of the past.

Against the backdrop of colorful advertisements for shampoos, contact lenses, lotions, and toothpaste, stylishly dressed and made-up young professional women walk purposefully past me, clutching knock-off Prada and Chanel purses. Amazing. They look no different than young, optimistic, and ambitious young women in other major cities around the world. I, on the other hand, look decidedly rumpled and not sleek in my faded jean shorts, 1986 5K fun run t-shirt, denim floppy hat, white athletic socks, and jogging shoes.

Given my "special" build, I skip the regular Chinese department stores and go to one that looks more Westernized to seek out that perfect bra. It possesses a simple interior décor, cleaner lines, dramatic colors, better merchandising, and a wide selection of imported Western goods that probably were made in China. On the third floor, I see a small selection of lacy bras, neatly arranged on tastefully spaced islands of metal racks. Three ladies dressed in matching powder-blue suits, neatly combed black hair, and carefully applied makeup approach me and ask if I need assistance.

Wow! Service. Customer service in China? Things have changed. Ah, that's right. This is a Japanese department store where service reigns supreme. In Chinglish, a mixture of English and street Mandarin, I tell the ladies what I am looking for.

I suffer a moment of indecision as I wait for the ladies to find some bras for me. I'm not going that far in my pursuit of beauty, am I? After all, I'm not disfiguring myself. Have I embarked on that slippery slope of beauty where one thing leads to another until my body is a jigsaw puzzle of tummy tucks, face-lifts, and liposuction marks? Is this how an addiction starts—first it's a made-to-order dress, then a bra to lift, a tube of lipstick to enhance, a blush and eyeliner to brighten, and then a shot of Botox to smooth? It's ironic that I feel insecure about my looks in China, my ancestral home, and feel the need for the trappings of the fashion industry.

I'm just getting a dress and a bra. That's it. Don't stress. Thankfully, the ladies quickly choose a few bras and pull me out of my panicked reverie. The young woman with her hair neatly pulled back in a ponytail shows me to a very small space to the right of the bra racks. Before I can close the door, the saleswoman pushes in after me and closes the door behind us. What is she doing? In my surprise, I can't say a word. This must be standard practice. I guess I'll let her stay.

Perhaps she thinks I'll steal the bra and she needs to watch me. Who knows? I take off my shirt and bra and lay them down to the right of me, on a chair. As I look back towards the mirror after taking my own bra off, I feel a hand on my breast. Her hand is on my breast!

I feel the coolness of her palm cup the curve at the bottom of my left breast. Heat sears my cheeks in embarrassment. I am absolutely dumbfounded and weirdly turned on at the same time. She pulls upward and stuffs me into the cup of the bra, holds me there while deftly doing the same with my right breast. She instructs me to hold myself up as she closes the clasp on the back.

A bra has never fit me so well. She compliments me on my figure. After an ego-bruising time at the dressmaker shop, my confidence is restored by her praise. Perhaps having an Eastern European build has its advantages in this country of slim people and new imported lingerie modeled on Western women. I don't even need any adjustments to my bra. I try on another one. This time, I politely decline her assistance as she reaches for my breast again. Hard to do when there's barely enough space to reach my arms in back of me.

I end up buying four bras, two of each kind. It's the most I have ever spent on bras. She assures me that this French label is of the highest quality. I believe her. I quickly make my purchase, thank her and the rest of the sales ladies. They must see the redness of my cheeks as I walk quickly away. I don't pause. I go down the escalator, down to the first floor, and out the door before I allow myself to think too deeply about what just happened. I laugh hysterically, dispelling the nervous energy and embarrassment built up inside me, causing a few people who passed me to whip back their heads to see what they missed.

How funny is it that I have to travel more than twelve thousand miles to find out certain truths about myself? I actually care that I'm huge in this country of smaller people (basketball star Yao Ming notwithstanding). I feel dowdy in my functional shorts, loose-fitting shirts, and cotton bras in fashionable Shanghai. And I want to look good. The hard part is admitting that I feel that way and that's O.K. I shake my head slightly and mull over this revelation. Then I smile as I walk back to the dressmaker to begin the prodding all over again, this time with the right bra.

Jacqueline C. Yau ate her first bowl of noodles on the road when she was three, traveling with her parents from California to Vancouver. Thus began a lifelong love of pasta and travel. When she is not curled up in a chair reading travel, romance, and adventure stories, she's sampling new cuisines, ricocheting down hiking trails, indulging her curiosity about all things, or laughing uproariously with family and friends. Her alter ego brings home the bacon as a strategic marketing consultant, drawing on her experiences as an Internet Keyword evangelist, brand manager, social entrepreneur, access cable TV host, and news reporter.

* * *

Ravioli, French Style

Some seasonings you really don't need.

"THERE IS A PUBIC HAIR IN MY PASTA," I SAID CALMLY, WITH as much dignity as I could muster. Across the table from me, Karen paused in mid-chew and put down the utensils, her eyes quickly scanning the surrounding diners for any undue attention. Perhaps they heard me say "pubic." We were in Grenoble, and people understood English very well. She carefully moved the silver pot of flowering lavender out of the way, leaned over the white-draped table and inspected the black, curly hair, complete with a white bulbous follicle, sitting on a freshly made goat cheese and spinach ravioli like an innocent bit of extra garnish. "Could be a chest hair," she said.

Karen is English and will suffer almost any humiliation quietly rather than make a fuss. "It's too curly for a chest hair. Could be from an arm pit, I will give you that," I said, raising a hand to get the waiter's attention. "Pit or crotch, I'm not going to eat it."

"You could just put it to one side," Karen suggested. The fingers of her right hand smoothed the napkin, ironed it against the table. "I mean, what are you hoping to achieve?"

English or not, in this instance she wasn't merely adhering to a genetic and cultural disposition for confrontation avoidance. Having lived in Grenoble for years, she had reason to question what greater good complaining would serve. In England or the U.S., apologies would have been forthcoming, as would a fresh portion or a different dish at no charge. But this was France and we both knew better.

Only three days earlier, on a cobblestone square in Aix-en-Provence, I had been served a salad with Lollo Rosso lettuce, artichoke hearts, pine nuts, and dirt. Not a modest little dusting of dirt crunching between my teeth, revealing a somewhat superficial rinsing, but a hearty clump of good, French soil. I could have grown cress in it. I showed the waitress, a wired thirtyish woman, expecting a modicum of remorse and a new salad. Instead I got an overbearing smile and *"C'est un peu de terre..."* It's a bit of dirt. What's all the fuss about? I insisted that the dirt should not be in my salad, so she looked at me as if I was a chihuahua having a yapping fit, tore off the ruffled lettuce leaf where the clump resided, and threw it on the ground in front of my sandaled feet. *"Voilà!"* Then she walked off to serve less demanding customers.

I generally prefer my salads without compost, and any type of hair in my food will dramatically reduce the chances of repeat business from me for the establishment in question. But I appreciate the lack of humility displayed by the average French service provider. Though occasionally counterproductive in the business sense of the word, it is at the very least honest. At best, it is what France is all about: a sense of equality and pride, a refusal to ingratiate. Compare this with the American cashier squeezing out a "Thank you for shopping at Walmart," when really he just wants you to pick up your change and exit his personal planet. American service is second to none when it comes to free water expediently delivered at the table, Disney smiles and verbal smoothies, but the pleasantries are often so forced and artificial that they leave you feeling more resented than by the irreverent French. Service is considered an unnecessary extra in France—a luxury reserved for the staggeringly rich and powerful. Ordinary people should not expect to be pampered, life is not for the cossetted or the easily deterred. Casual disdain is part of the experience, an enthusiastically served meal belongs in Greece or Italy, not France. The liquid mix of charm and superiority that characterizes the hotel receptionist, the boutique owner, the greengrocer, is a language of its own: of sighs, pregnant pauses, slow feline gestures, and shamelessly verbose eyebrows.

Familiar with this language, I was not expecting heartfelt apologies or faces burning with humiliation at my presentation of the hair, even in the relatively expensive restaurant where Karen and I were dining on the evening in question. Setting myself what I considered a realistic goal, I was aiming for a replacement portion, sans pubes. After many unsuccessful attempts at making eye contact, I managed to attract the attention of our whiskered headwaiter who floated over and asked with a half-smile what he could do for me. I pointed out the curled-up evidence. He sighed and looked at me like he would love to help and was saddened by the fact that he could not, as if I had just asked him to donate a kidney. He shook his slick, dark head slowly and said, "It is not mine..."

Rikke Jorgensen is a freelance writer who has traveled Europe, Australia, New Zealand, Africa, and North America extensively. She is addicted to dogs, and lives in San Francisco.

THOMAS GOLTZ

* * *

A Bard in the Bush

Kenyans know culture when they see it.

ENTER Stage Right, The Bard, A Younge American Youthe Of Naive Aspecte. He Carryeth A Shoulder Bagge Filled With Sundry Stuffe, Including A DOZEN WOODEN PUPPET FIGURINES And Severale WOODEN MASQUES.

Next Enter Stage Left, The CROWDE, Which Consisteth of Divers Folke of the Streete Varietee, The Majority Of Whom Are Blackamoors. They Banter and Joke Until The Bard Calleth for Silence, Upon Which Time The Bard Slippeth A Masque Over His Countenance Whilst Placing A Seconde Masque Upon The Pavement, Thus Creating A Body. Alarums Sound; A Long Trumpet Flourisheth (it is actually a bus), And The Bard Continues, Now Bellowing Over the Trafficke:

> Friends, Romans, Countrymen—lend me your ears!
> I come to bury Caesar, not to praise him
> The evil that men do live after them
> The good is oft interred with their bones...

179

★

It is Marc Antony eulogizing the Caesar, in a soliloquy that many might recognize from an annual Shakespeare In The Park production. Myself, I had to memorize parts of that speech in English class with Mr. Jacobsen, at Shanely High School, Fargo, North Dakota. Mr. Jacobsen. He was mainly a basketball coach and didn't know too much about Shakespeare or scansion, but he had a good sense of humor, and gave you extra credit on the vocabulary test if you gave the answer "a couple of doctors" as the definition of "paradox." I wonder what he would think about his guy bellowing iambic pentameter over the growling traffic? Extra credit for public exhibitionism? Why not?

The noble Brutus hath informed you
That Caesar was ambitious

But I am not in Fargo. Being a trained observer I have noticed, for example, that the weather is sticky hot, not bone-numbing cold. Also, most of the audience gathered to hear the Bard are black and not white—and the only black man I knew in North Dakota was Michael Collins, Christian Brother principal of Shanley High School.

In fact, I have determined that the venue is the pavement outside New Stanley Hotel in Nairobi, Kenya, a place once frequented by the literary likes of Ernest Hemingway, Alan Moorehead, and Robin Ruack. I rather doubt, however, if any of these Grand Old Men of African Literature would feel comfortable here and now. In the main the crowd gathered on the pavement in front of their old haunt consists of shoe-shine boys, ladies of the night caught out during the cruel light of day, and a few Japanese and German tourists peeking over the rim of the crowd with shit-eating grins plastered on their faces. A couple of pickpockets and petty thieves are also on hand, working the outside of the crowd. One of them is even now sneaking a stealthy hand toward the Bard's collection bowl, primed with his own cast to encourage the assembled to toss in a coin or two. The Bard sees this, too, and steps on the young thief's fingers without breaking scansion, resulting in a collective howl from the crowd:

> You all did love him once, not without cause—
> What cause withholds you then to mourn for him?
> Oh, Judgment! Thou art fled to brutish beasts
> And men have lost their reason! Bear with me,
> For my heart is in the coffin there with Caesar
> And I must pause 'til it come back to me…

The Bard is now taking a bow. A horn honks and a collective cough seems to ripple through the audience. The three or four tourists who stopped to listen are walking down the street with smirks on their faces, having made no movement toward donating any money into the collection. A cigarette butt flies by the Bard's nose, followed by a paper cup.

"Thank you very much," says the Bard. "Are there now any requests?"

A murmur passes through the throng, and a large, well-dressed African man steps forward. He is dressed in a three-piece suit, with the button of the ruling political party pinned to the jacket lapel, and he is smiling far too sweetly to bode any relief.

"Yes, *bwana*," says the man, using the form of address employed by colonial black servants towards their colonial white masters. "My request is that you stop."

A howl of delight rises from those gathered along the street, and the crowd presses in closer to eavesdrop on the conversation.

"Why?" asks the Bard, pathetically.

"Why?" the interloper asks rhetorically in an even louder voice. "Brothers!" he thunders. "The *bwana* asks us why he should stop! Brothers! He should stop not because he is bad, which he is, but mainly because we all had to memorize that same speech in school at the knee of colonial schoolmarms and masters! And what does that speech have to do with Africa? Shakespeare is English and we are not!!"

The feckless crowd roars its approval, and the Bard seems to cringe beneath his mask.

"*Bwana* Brutus," the man continues. "You are like the missionary of Shakespeare, come to take away our African culture! Go back to you own country and leave Africa for the Africans and Kenya for the Kenyans!…"

I'd want to help the Bard but I cannot. He has gotten himself in this mess and will have to get himself out, by himself. For a year and a half, he has been a self-styled Johnny Appleseed of Shakespeare in Africa, surviving by his wits and élan. But now he is too tired, physically and emotionally, to even consider countering the attack being made on him. In fact, he is about to snap. It is time to duck, collect his props, pack his bags and go—and the sooner the better.

The crowd has grown bored and started to disperse, with the exception of the jowly man in the three-piece suit, who stands triumphantly over the Bard, arms akimbo. Then a young street kid drops a shilling into the Bard's collection bowl.

Clink, goes the coin, and the Bard looks up.

"Please, *bwana*, you play Macbethi?" the young urchin tentatively asks.

"Not now," mutters the Bard, trying to shut out the world.

"I see you do Macbethi last year, *mzuri sana*," says the lad, and smiles.

The young patron is dressed in what would generously be described as rags. His feet are without shoes, and his pants are too large and filled with holes and held up with a belt made of string. He produces another brass shilling and drops it on top of the first donation, resulting in another meek jingle of appreciation.

"Ha!" It is the fat politician in the three-piece suit again, his Rolex watch weighing heavy on the street kid's scrawny shoulders. "Not only does this *bwana* mean to rob us of our national culture, but he also means to steal the hard-earned savings of this young citizen! Don't let them eat bread! Let them eat Shakespeare! *Hahaha*!!"

"You eat Shakespeare," says the street urchin, writhing away from the fat man's embrace. "You too fat, anyway!"

"You make good Falstaff," adds an anonymous voice and a snicker runs through the throng, followed by a chanting chorus, "Falstaff, Falstaff, you play Falstaff!"

They are not referring to the Bard. Dysentery from Capetown to Cairo has long robbed him of any claim to play Falstaff. They are now mocking the interloper, who is fat.

"What do you know about Shakespeare," sneers the suit-man, turning on the remnants of the crowd. "Half of you cannot even read English!"

"Jules Nyerre write Julius Caesar in Swahili," someone says. The Tanzanian leader's brand of African Socialism has always made the post-colonial Kenyan elite nervous.

"Macbethi!" someone else demands, and another coin is tossed at the collection bowl. It hits the fat man in the three-piece suit on the head. A howl of laughter erupts from the crowd, which is taking its pleasure at the expense of the politician, and not the Bard.

"Macbeth, Macbeth, Macbeth!" chants the crowd, and a small shower of coins lands over the Bard and his tormentor, with those that bounce off into the street hotly pursued by the younger thieves and urchins, who then sling their windfall profits back at the stage. "Macbeth! Macbeth! Macbeth!"

"Yes, please, do perform that scene you do from Macbeth," says a well-dressed African woman who has now come forward, pressing a paper note into the Bard's hand. "It is certainly apropos today, given the state of affairs in Congo."

"Down with dictators!" crows the crowd, demanding action.

"I shall call the police!" bellows the fat man, in a last ditch effort to stop the show. But it is too late. There are several policemen in the audience, waiting for the curtain to rise, and Bard is already digging for the *panga* blade in his performance bag that serves as the knife used to dispatch the doomed King Duncan.

Is this a dagger I see before me?
The handle toward my hand?

If the changed mood of the crowd is not enough, the appearance of the *panga* in the hands of the man wearing the mask is: the interloper leaps from the stage with a yelp, while the restored audience roars its approval and initiates yet another shower of coin.

Come, let me clutch thee—
I have thee not and yet I see thee still...

Now the crowd is silent, attentive. Only the grinding gears

of a bus out on Kenyatta Avenue break the silence of the street-side stage. The Bard has received a reprieve, a second life, a second wind as he follows the upheld dagger around the stage, feet miming disturbed steps down cold castle stones.

> Art thou not, fatal vision, as sensible
> To feeling as to sight? Or art thou but
> A dagger of the mind, a false conception
> Proceeding from the heat-oppressed brain…

His meter is intact, caesuras, too. The Bard may be leaving Africa the next day, but he will have his farewell performance. His voice, which had felt weak and graveled before, is now responding as if he had trained it in Greco-Roman amphitheaters and not African streets, which may be the same thing, when all is said and done. The crowd has grown silent and attentive, tying the classical texts into concrete, local experience. They have all seen coups and counter-coups and known unexplained assassinations. They may not understand every word, but every nuance is as familiar as last year's leader.

> While I threat, he lives
> Words to the heat of deeds too cold breath gives!
> I go and it is done; the bell invites me.
> Hear it not Duncan, for it is a knell
> That summons thee to heaven—or to hell!

A flourish, then a bow. Hoots and hollers. But the Bard knows it is applause. It washes over the young man like a magic balm, ointment for the cuts and nicks and gashes applied to his fragile ego over eighteen months on the road in deepest, darkest Africa.

"Thank you, thank you," says the Bard, now speaking in something closer to the Midwestern twang of American English than the round, quasi-Elizabethan accent of Caesar and Macbeth. "For any of you who would like to help me get out of Africa the way I came in, please! Put money in my purse!"

With another flourish and bow, the Bard reaches toward the crowd with his collection plate in one hand, while removing the Masai mask with the other.

I am stunned. Through the haze of twenty years I recognize this man. He is young and thinner and certainly has more hair on his head—but he is me.

Thomas Goltz is a Shakespearean actor and author. This story was excerpted from his manuscript, A Bard in the Bush or Assassinating Shakespeare: The True Confessions of a One-Man Wandering Bard in an Africa. *He lives in Montana.*

KEN VOLLMER

✦ ✦ ✦

Underpants from Hell

What's going on down there?

THOSE WHO ARE SQUEAMISH MAY WANT TO PASS OVER THIS tale of woe, for it addresses a topic that many fear to broach and others will discuss only in hushed voices. In short: the seedy world of undergarments.

Many travelers find it important to have quality underwear for their journeys. Maybe they rely on the moisture-wicking properties of the latest synthetics while hiking. Or they mandate that comfort is key and insist only that their drawers feel nice. Perhaps they pack something a little lacy, hoping for a scandalous interlude on the road. But undoubtedly, lest their mothers die of shame in the event of a serious accident, their panties, boxers, and briefs must be clean and new.

At the dawn of a recent trip to Japan, I opted to test-drive the latest in high-performance underwear, the sort of stuff that promises to keep you comfortably dry at all times while looking flashy and rescuing hostages from terrorists. (That's right—the underwear does the rescuing. You're just along for the ride. It's that good.) Knowing that my underlayer would protect me even if I charged through a lava flow gave me the confidence I needed to take the world by storm.

Unfortunately, it was a smelly storm indeed. While proponents of synthetic, high-performance underwear make no false claims as to its numerous advantages over normal stock, there is one category in which tech-knickers advocates are conspicuously tight-lipped: odor.

For the record, I am not, by nature or habit, a malodorous person. But after a day of light hiking on the streets of Kyoto in my dread under-apparel, I unwittingly developed a personal aroma that was startlingly foul. The scent was so mighty that it practically had a personality. It could only be described as *stench*. Sadly, I didn't realize any of this until I went indoors.

As I sat down in a café to relax for a few minutes, I thought at first that I had made a terrible mistake in assessing the cleanliness of the establishment—a wisp of unpleasant air reached my nostrils just a few moments after I parked myself in a comfy armchair. The smell was completely alien, an unsettling blend of body odor, petrochemicals, and rotten laundry, peppered with the tang of a burning fish-packing facility.

I scanned the other customers, but no one else seemed to notice anything amiss. Certainly none of them seemed a likely candidate to be ground zero of such a stink. It occurred to me to check the bottom of my shoes on the chance that I'd stepped in something—I hadn't. I reluctantly attributed the toxic atmosphere to clashing societal standards (though Japan had seemed a conscientiously hygienic place until that point) and resolved to pay it no mind. I ordered a cup of coffee.

But the fell reek would not retire. Instead, it redoubled its noxious efforts. The odor was so powerful that I half expected to find it had visibly manifested as tendrils of fetid, ochre mist snaking through the room. I couldn't possibly be the only one to notice.

Sure enough, by this time a few of the other café patrons were looking around with tell-tale nose-scrunched facial expressions. As I considered their various positions in hopes of triangulating the source of this brutal olfactory offense, they seemed to focus their attention. *On me.*

I reached the shocking conclusion at the same time they did: *I* was the source of the loathsome stink. So quick to assume my unassailable innocence, I hadn't realized my own role as the prototypical barbarian. *I was a smelly foreigner.*

I left the money for my undelivered drink on the table and hastily exited the café, studiously avoiding eye contact with those who had so embarrassingly come to know me. I proceeded directly home, walking only the most wind-swept avenues, and there burned the offending undergarments in an incense-laden ritual of redemption. I stowed my other high-tech briefs deep in my backpack, for use only in the event that I needed to scare off wild animals.

Ken Vollmer is the author of The Wanderlust Survival Guide: Tips and Tales for World Travel, *a compendium of travel wisdom and stories of his comic misadventures (www.wanderlustguide.com). When he isn't recklessly throwing himself in the path of international incidents, he guides walking tours of San Francisco for Hostelling International.*

✳ ✳ ✳

Beating the Water with an Expensive Stick

Do they really pay good money to do that?

IT WAS A FASCINATING SIGHT: MEN STANDING AROUND IN rubber pants, adjusting their flies, whipping their rods back and forth, and occasionally exclaiming, "Look here. I've got a big one!"

Of course, I'm talking about fly-fishing. And here in the shadow of Pikes Peak, Colorado, fly-fishing isn't just a hobby, it's a way of life.

I, too, was wearing rubber pants, also known as "waterproof support hose," as I stood in the parking lot of Deckers, a well-fished stream just twenty minutes north of Pikes Peak, waiting for my 9 A.M. beginners' fly-fishing class to start.

I spent a good deal of time checking my gear, or just fidgeting with it. I carried my rented $300 rod and reel awkwardly, like a new father trying to find a comfortable position to hold his baby. I spent ten minutes studying my sunglasses, trying to determine whether or not they were polarized because I had been told it was a crucial feature. And I rechecked the new fishing license I had picked up at 7-Eleven for $5 to make sure it had the right date and to see if there was a coupon on the back for a Big Gulp.

Fellow classmates Carol and Libby, both in their forties, arrived together. Mark, also around forty, and the only one who confessed any experience, came on his own.

Our barrel-chested, bearded instructor was also named Mark, but for purposes of clarification, I'll just refer to him as Instructor Mark. Instructor Mark was leading the class with Antonio, a junior high-school teacher and part-time fishing guide. Both of these men were wearing vests covered with several hundred dollars worth of fly-fishing gizmos, though to the untrained eye it just looked like they were wearing colorful wads of lint.

Instructor Mark announced that we would start fishing with nymphs. This didn't do much in the way of explanation because neither Libby, Carol, nor myself would have been able to pick a nymph out of a police lineup, even if everyone but the nymph was wearing a police uniform. Quite simply, Instructor Mark explained, a nymph stays underwater, not on top of it, and nymphs should *definitely* not be confused with streamers, emergers, wet flies, or dry flies (whatever those were).

To determine exactly what sort of nymph we needed, Instructor Mark took a ping-pong net, or something that looked like a ping-pong net but probably cost ten times as much, and used it as a strainer to collect some debris floating in the river. He pulled up a couple of squirmy critters the size of head lice and studied them with more interest than you'd expect a grown man to display when looking at aquatic larvae. This, he explained (as if it weren't evident), was part of the fun of fly-fishing.

Antonio baited his line with one of these creatures and caught a trout to show us how it's done. More impressive than the catch, which took him about a minute, was how gentle he was with the fish once he had caught it. He wet his hands before touching it so he wouldn't damage its scales, and he extracted the fly like a thoracic surgeon. Then he held the trout in the water and stroked it while it regained its strength. All of this would have been quite touching if Antonio hadn't just jerked the fish to shore by its mouth with a hook.

The whole process seemed a bit like lassoing a bird flying south for the winter and yanking it to the ground, then fluffing up its feathers and letting it go. It just didn't look like that much fun for the trout, some of which, Instructor Mark explained, had been caught more than *forty times*.

I must have caught one of these professional trout. The moment I got him on the line, he swam straight to shore and beached himself. He knew the drill. He didn't even blink when we took a flash photo of me holding him. Possibly because he didn't have eyelids.

I caught two trout and hooked myself three times (twice on my shirt and once on my hat). Libby and Carol each caught two trout, plus each other. And even Signe, who put down her camera for twenty minutes, caught two fish and Libby's shirt. Mark the student was having bad luck, probably because he jinxed himself by telling everyone he had experience.

I have to admit, it felt good to pull in a fish, to see the line jerk and the trout jump out of the water. I felt a bit like Brad Pitt in the movie *A River Runs through It*.[1] But when I had to reach down to get the hook out of the trout, it didn't quite seem worth the fish's discomfort. Especially when he wriggled out of my hands and fell on a rock. I can certainly understand the appeal of fishing, though. Particularly when extremely expensive speedboats are involved.

---

[1] Except, of course, that I'm a little taller.

The fish we caught were called rainbow trout and brown trout. The rainbows were imported from California and the browns were brought in from Germany. I began to wonder what I was doing in Colorado, aside from sponging off my old college roommate, Tim, for a few days.

Tim, an experienced fly-fisherman, had witnessed my casting and told me, with that honesty one reserves for good friends, I was "whacking water with a stick." To learn to appreciate another aspect of the sport, I let Tim try to teach me to tie a fly.

This was confusing right from the start. The size of the lines and hooks get smaller as the numbers that describe them get bigger. Each fly-tying tool has a complex name, and the only thing more complex than the name of the tool is the name of the fly you're trying to tie with it. At least, when in doubt, you can call any lure a "fly"—even lures that stay underwater, look like worms, and have less chance of achieving flight than a hypoglycemic hippopotamus.

"Here," Tim would say. "This is the little doohickie. And this is the big doohickie. You just hold this chicken feather and wrap this 22-pound line around—Doug, keep watching—and make this loop. Then you just—Doug, see how easy this is?—tuck this thingy under here while letting the little number 14 doohickie hang. You see that, right?" And I would tell Tim, "Yes, I saw it." Then he'd hand me the tools and I'd just sit there, thinking I would have a better chance of constructing a Boeing 747.

After one hour, Tim had talked me through making a "ten-minute" fly. It looked very artistic…in a Picasso sort of way. There appeared to be two heads, two abdomens, and several stray appendages. Tim and Signe just stared at it, not quite sure what to say. Perhaps, I suggested, it might perform well in the streams near Chernobyl.

Doug Lansky is a nationally-syndicated travel columnist, correspondent for Public Radio's "Savvy Traveler," Discovery Channel host, author of Last Trout in Venice *(from which this story was excerpted),* The Rough Guide to First-Time Around the World, *and editor of the award-winning travel humor anthology,* There's No Toilet Paper on the Road Less Traveled. *Doug spends most of his time in Europe with his Swedish wife, Signe, a medical doctor, and their young daughter.*

✦ ✦ ✦

Boxcar Steve

*Some adventures are freighted with meaning,
just not the one you'd planned on.*

"WHEN I WAS FREIGHT TRAIN HOPPING…" HE BEGAN HIS story. That was all I needed to hear. The wheels of adventure spun inside my head like a 4X4 Jeep stuck in the mud. I didn't remember anything else that night except for the Bloody Mary mussels that I ravished while the rest of the dinner party sat enthralled with his story. I waited for my chance to demand his railroad tutelage.

He was Richard Sterling, the Indiana Jones of Gastronomy. The Fearless Diner. A travel writer and editor nearly twice my age of twenty-four. Richard was a storyteller who liked the sound of his own voice, and whose best stories involved his daring global escapades in grub, drink, love, and war.

"Take me," I announced. "I've always wanted to hop a freight train." Truth. Word up. No shit.

"They don't let women in the yard," Richard warned.

"I'll dress as a man." I wiped off my lipstick.

"They'll roll you if they find out," he declared showing his command of the hobo vernacular.

"All the better for my story," I argued, uncrossing my legs and planting my hands on my hips.

"If we run into bulls, it could get dicey."

"When can we leave?" I said, putting the discussion to rest. I could leave my job as a nanny for about three days. "Wait, what's a bull?"

A month later I woke up on the floor, one of several bodies in the aftermath of a house party. My lover's hand caressed my upper thigh and began its way down the length of my leg. I jerked my body from him just as he reached the soft forest I had cultivated on my calf.

"What's this?" he asked knowing full well that I was no hippie.

"I stopped shaving to make my disguise as a man more authentic."

"You what?"

"I'm going to hop a freight train. The guy who's taking me said they frown upon women in the hobo jungles," I explained, matter-of-factly, as if describing how to operate a washing machine.

"Boxcar Leo!" my lover announced, and the room burst into uproarious laughter.

"Richard is going to call me Steve."

One week and two trips to Goodwill later, I met Richard at Oakland's piggyback tracks. We had agreed to come at dusk in our worst clothing. I had spent hours concocting my outfit. This was the real deal, no phony Halloween garb. Erasing all traces of femininity, I taped my breasts, donned scuffed men's work boots, torn corduroy trousers, a faded navy blue sweatshirt, and a wool ski cap. An empty ten-pound coffee can and patched up pillow hung by rope from the bottom of my pack.

Richard arrived dressed as if he were going to an alumni football game. He wore khaki pants, a Pendleton overcoat, and a spotless Cal Berkeley hat. I berated him for not lowering himself to the occasion. He asked me if I'd brought the salmon.

Yes, I had. Suddenly, the fact that I was a woman no longer seemed an issue. If any of the other hoboes found out that we had packed a feast of salmon and champagne for brunch, we'd certainly get jumped.

Richard left me sitting on a utility box while he went looking for an open car. The idea was to get on the car while it was still, and wait for it to move later in the night. In his absence I thought through how I'd use the coffee can as my toilet. I just hoped I didn't have to go number two.

As the night grew darker and Richard hadn't returned, I wondered where the other hoboes were. We were open to going anywhere, but wanted to get picked up by a train headed northeast towards Roseville, a central hobo jungle outside of Sacramento.

"They thought I was their boss," chuckled Richard when he got back. "I walked up to the men working on the tracks, they said they were going as fast as they could."

"See, I told you that you didn't look like a hobo."

"They also showed me which tracks would be moving tonight, let's go." I followed him a few hundred yards. The tracks were like a ten-lane highway of parked steel and rust: brown cars, black cars, most covered with graffiti, and cars with no walls, just the flat bed. We picked one of two open boxcars and looked north up the tracks, confident that we would be moving in no time. The yard was quiet but sure to pick up activity.

Richard told me that the open boxcars get mighty dusty and to put on my bandana, thief style. It would protect me from breathing in too much dirt. I dutifully obeyed.

Then he reached into his pack and got out the gin and tonic. We toasted to Lady Luck and threw a few back.

"Steve, wake up!" Richard jostled me, "It's 8:30. Steve, you should see yourself, you're covered in filth."

He laughed. I sat up and got my bearings. My ass hurt and the bandana was still on. I was covered in a film of dust from head to toe. I stood and shook it off like a wet dog air-dries. The King of the Road was sparkling clean.

"Where are we?" I asked.

"Oakland," Richard fumed. "The car didn't move all night. I'm surprised you could sleep, trains were whizzing by."

I left my coffee can in the car and hopped out for a pee. Since the car wasn't moving, it was just as easy to pull down my pants and do it while leaning against the hitch in back.

We climbed onto the open car across from us and started to play cards. Four hours later we were bored with talk, waiting, and the hobo life. The car still hadn't moved. The only thing that could lift our spirits was brunch. Richard popped the cork on the champagne while I covered our baguettes with cream cheese and pink Alaskan fillets.

In going through my bag I found the cell phone that my girlfriend had insisted I take for an emergency. Richard wanted to call some culinary friends and tell them what we were eating and where we were. Just as he started to dial, there was a huge jolt to our car. We grabbed our drinks before our car was hit with another crash and started to move.

"Woohoo!" we yelped, and slapped a high five. Now we were getting somewhere. Richard stuck his head out the car as the train slowly crept north. A hundred feet up the track a rail worker manned a post. Richard waved at him in a salute of success. The worker waved back. Then, there was another jolt, and we were thrown back. The car stopped moving.

"They decoupled us," Richard said, deflated.

"They what?"

"They hooked up the cars they needed and took off without us."

We'd been on the tracks for nineteen hours, and hadn't traveled but a few hundred feet, not miles. The sun was high in the sky and I'd already taken off half my disguise.

"Should we call for a ride?" I asked.

"Nah, there's a bar within walking distance. Let's get a drink."

"Yeah," I agreed, a stiff one sounded about right. On the way I could call my bosses and assure them their nanny hadn't been rolled.

Jennifer L. Leo is the editor of the bestselling Sand in My Bra and Other Misadventures: Funny Women Write from the Road *and co-editor of* A Woman's Path: Women's Best Spiritual Travel Writing. *Her web site, WrittenRoad.com, is an online resource for travel writers. Richard was the first person to invite her to dinner parties that included travel guidebook writers and magazine publishers. He still calls her Steve.*

* * *

Saigon Games

Take that, you scoundrel!

SAIGON HAS ALWAYS BEEN A LADY, AND A BEAUTIFUL ONE, BUT a lady with a touch of sin. There is a game you can play here when you are tired of more mundane pastimes and hanker after a contest of wits and nerve. It is not inherently danger-ous, but neither is it a game for the faint of heart. Much is at stake. For in this game the hunted becomes the hunter, and the predator turns prey. I should say that there is currently an Englishwoman residing at the 333 Hotel with her left leg in a cast for a torn ligament. But her's is the only injury I have ever heard of. And she played at three o'clock in the morn-ing after an evening of drinking. And she played rough. Many beginners do. I did.

So you must not play this game when you have been drinking, or ill, or in a bad mood. Your senses and your reflexes, and your powers of observation and decision must be in top form, because you, the visitor, the amateur, will be going up against the pros. But you can win at this game. If you follow my advice and learn from me you can win almost every time. In fact, I haven't lost yet. Although in fairness I'd have to say that the outcome of my most recent encounter was very dodgy and too close for comfort. And I had put too much at stake. But I won. The game is called Trolling for Pickpockets.

Trolling for pickpockets, as a Saigonese contact sport, was invented during the Tet New Year celebrations of 1992 by Bruce and Paul Harmon and myself. We were wandering the Ben Thanh market on Le Thanh Ton Boulevard one fine morning. The holiday crowd was dense and there was much rubbing of shoulders. Two unsavory looking guys walking side by side approached me head on. I knew I was their mark. Their appearance alone tipped me off. The best players look like the woodwork. Just before contact they parted like waters and went to both sides of me, bracketing me hard. I felt hands as they slid by.

I am very aware of hands in this country. In Vietnam it is impolite and unseemly to touch strangers. Most people don't even observe the Western custom of shaking hands. Children will sometimes touch you as you walk by, out of childish curiosity at someone who looks nothing like them or theirs. Or they will run up from behind, touch you and flee. But they're just playing a game of "counting coup." They know it's naughty, but the fascination of foreigners overcomes their good manners. Or they might be pickpockets in training. But certainly an adult who touches you on the street is at least being disrespectful, and could be trying to get your goods.

So that morning in the market when I felt hands, my own right hand went instinctively to the small bag I carry on my hip, slung to my belt like a holster. My hand brushed a strange hand that instantly snapped away. At the same time my left hand, almost of its own accord, shot through an undulating press of bodies and grabbed a fistful of shirt front. The guy on my right melted into the crowd. But on my left I gave a tug and jerked the wearer of the shirt to front and center. I relieved him of my sunglasses. Maintaining my grip on his shirt I told him in no uncertain looks and tone that I would eat him without salt if he should make me his mark again.

At this point Bruce and Paul, having seen what happened in the brief encounter, came rushing to my aid, ready to help me pound the culprit into the dirt like a railroad spike. But I let the lad go, sent him back to school to study his lessons a little harder. After all, he had nothing of mine. And I had one of his shirt buttons. To my amazement I wasn't even angry at him. I felt no sense of outrage at the attempt on my person and property. I had no desire to haul the bad guy off to the pokey and demand justice. I didn't thirst for his blood. Rather, I was jazzed. Yessss! I was pumped. I was mighty. I had won.

"Richard," Paul said. "That was beautiful. You caught that guy like a fly ball!"

And Bruce said, "Damn it! I want to catch one too!"

And so the sport of trolling for pickpockets came into being. We immediately set our hooks with bait: sunglasses, banknotes, pens, and so on hanging provocatively from our pockets. And then we went watchfully on patrol. Bruce was the first to bag one. He was a solo operator who foolishly went for Bruce's front pocket, the most easily defensible. Obviously a rank beginner, and Bruce should take no undue pride in hooking him. Bruce's response to the guy? No shirt-grabbing or nasty looks of intimidation. Just an openhanded straight right to the chest. Doesn't sound like much, but Bruce is a powerful man. It sent the cutpurse three or four steps back and almost onto his ass. A troupe of cyclo drivers lounging nearby saw the encounter and nearly rolled on the ground laughing. Cyclo drivers are poor, and nightclub entertainment is beyond their means. But Bruce had amused them mightily. So much so that they wanted more. Knowing who some of the local pickpockets were, they encouraged them to try their wiles on us. We all bagged our limit, and by midafternoon the Ben Than market was cleansed of pick-pockets, and the people were secure.

Paul had the most dramatic capture. As we were new to the game we didn't know that skillful players can get through even the strongest lines of defense in the forms of buttons, zippers, locks, and so on. Only the most alert vigilance is proof against a good player. The brotherhood of cutpurses and pickpockets even has a saying on the subject: "You can't steal a man's goods when he's thinking about them."

Paul carries his expensive camera in a holster with Velcro, buttons, and a zipper to secure it. Seems safe. But a senior member of the opposing team actually got through the defenses, grabbed the camera, and was on the lam by the time Paul realized what was up. He gave chase with a hue and cry. Bruce and I followed about twenty paces behind. We ran passed the cyclo drivers, who cheered us on. We ran passed the fabric merchants who cursed us for the disruption. Rounding a corner into the food stalls, Paul was closing in when the thief lost his breath, or heart for the chase, or just slipped on a banana peel. He went crashing into a stall selling deep-fried spring rolls. His impact knocked over a huge wok full of bubbling hot oil which spilled down his back, across his ass, and down his thighs. In an instant he was airborne. Almost before his feet touched the ground he was gone in a flash, leaving behind Paul's camera, the echoes of his screams, and a curious odor reminiscent of deep-fried pork skins.

Crowned with many victories we repaired to our digs at the Prince hotel, at that time a favorite of backpackers and other budget travelers such as we were on that occasion. We told everyone then gathered in the bar of our exploits. But they were not amused or impressed. A pious Swede even scolded us. "You shouldn't do that," he complained. "These people are poor!"

"And they're gonna stay that way if they try to make a living out of our pockets," Bruce said.

"But they're socialists!" the Swede cried.

"Huh? What? Socialist thieves?" Paul wondered aloud.

"Socialists!" the man reiterated, trying to get it through to us why it was a bad thing to toy with commie crooks.

"Hey," I asked him, "with that kind of individual initiative and free-enterprise spirit, wouldn't that make them capitalists?"

The Swede shook his head in despair. The backpackers shifted uncomfortably in their printed t-shirts and Indian-made, cotton pajama-style trousers. They tugged at their blond dreadlocks and stared into their watery budget beer and thin herbal teas.

Note to players: Don't share this game with backpackers or Swedes. They have no fire in the belly. Australians make good players. Any nation that has an annual dwarf-tossing contest will make good players. Texans and Yorkshiremen are good for trolling. As are Nepalis, especially if they have a bit of Ghurka background. I spent a pleasant afternoon last week with a guy from Ghana. He told me that he plays the game at home! (I guess it's like the wheel: been invented many times.) I suppose it's not so much where people come from that counts the most. It's that gleam in their eye that tells you who will make a player.

Now I don't want you to get the idea that Saigon is a dangerous place. In fact it's one of the safest cities you can visit. Far safer than San Francisco, Los Angeles, or New York. I can nearly guarantee that you won't get shot in Saigon (unless it's by the authorities); that you will not get raped (unless you pay someone to do it); that you will not be hit on the head and have your poke pinched; you won't be kidnapped, murdered, stabbed, gassed, poisoned, or fed bad food. This is generally a nonviolent society. The criminal urge is expressed in the con, the counterfeit, the card sharp, the stock swindle, the pickpocket, and the cutpurse.

Now there are exceptions to every rule, and one of them hangs out near my hotel. I've recognized him as a player and a mean sort, too. We've never spoken but we have exchanged some hostile glances as I've passed by his station. We know each other, and we both know we know. A few days ago he made an attempt on me as I made my way home.

I was hot and tired and in no mood to play. For the first time in all my encounters I got angry. As soon as I felt him make his move I wheeled around and threw up my fists in a proper boxing stance and challenged him to "Try it again if you dare, you SOB!" At the same instant he assumed a kung fu–type pose, curled up with one foot off the ground, ready to release a kick. We had a standoff for about two or three seconds, and we had begun to draw attention when I decided that he had just rendered a good performance. Most pickpockets would have slunk away at the prospect of a punch in the nose. I laughed and offered him my hand, and we shook. Then I turned to go and the creep tried me again! I swung around to backhand him, but by then he was gone. Fast man. Dangerous player. But I still won.

In playing this game the ideal conclusion to any encounter is so subtle that only you and your fish know that it happened. You troll through a market or fair or promenade where you know that they school. Your baited hook is out, not too obviously but temptingly. (And of course you're not carrying anything you can't afford to lose.) Your senses are heightened. You see, hear, even smell with intense acuity. You are very much alive to all around you. You watch for any unusual or sudden movement, especially at the periphery of your vision. You listen for sounds of breathing and the rustle of clothing or bags, or the soft footfalls that tell you it's about to happen. But most of all your sense of touch is so acute that you can feel odors afloat on the air. You're aware of the slightest change in temperature. You know the texture, weight and fit of your clothing. For it's your tactile faculties that will most likely tell you that the hand is at your pocket and you've just hooked your fish.

You now have one, maybe two seconds at most, to win the game. That's not much time, but it's you who has the advantage of surprise. Your quarry doesn't know that you've been lying in wait for him. He thinks you're easy pickings. So now! Wheel around! Make your move small and without show, but make it sudden and swift for the fright it will give him. Grab for the wrist whose hand has your bait and hold firmly because he may try to bolt. The trick is not to wrestle with him, but to make eye contact as soon as possible. Nine times out of ten it will make him freeze. He knows the jig is up, might even realize he's been had. And being the nonviolent, nonconfrontational sort that he is, he submits. You hold him for a second or two, just for emphasis. And just to appreciate his racing pulse. Then you quietly let him go. Just catch and release. He'll scurry off to hide somewhere, perhaps to be cuffed and scolded by his master who was watching from a fair vantage point. Score one for the visitors. Yesss!

There is one class of pickpocket that bears warning of. He is the same type that provided the Englishwoman in the 333 Hotel with a cast for her leg. He is known as a "cowboy." He rides a motorbike with an accomplice passenger behind known as "the snatch." They ride up alongside you, usually from behind, and grab whatever protrudes, then they're off across town. Because of their speed, power, and clever tactics they are the worst you'll ever go up against. The trick with them is simply to step aside as they pass and let the snatch grab nothing but air.

But when a cowboy and his snatch made their move upon the Englishwoman she was feeling cocky, and thought she could drop the snatch to the ground by hanging on tight to her boodle. But at 3 a.m. and full of drink she was in no shape for combat. They dragged her for a few yards until she let go and slammed into a tree. She cursed them loudly, and if their feelings were hurt it would be a good thing. Now she plots a better game, while the cowboy and his snatch live well.

In all my years in Southeast Asia I never once personally encountered a cowboy. Until last week. I was in a cyclo driven by a guy I hire often. He's a good guy with a sense of humor and we get along well. I can't pronounce his name, nor he mine, so I call him Joe. He calls me Kieu. I don't know if my spelling is correct, and he can't tell me because he's illiterate, but I'm sure it's close enough.

We had stopped at an intersection for a traffic light. The light was just about to turn green, and I could feel Joe taking a strain on the pedals of his cyclo, preparing for the mad free-for-all that Saigon traffic is. Cars, motorbikes, and cyclos lined up behind us were doing the same.

I am blessed with good vision. It's 20/10, which means that I can see twice as far as most people. I'm also just an observant sort of guy. Most writers are. I saw to my right on the cross street, and heading into the intersection, a red and white motorbike driven by a t-shirt clad man, and another riding pillion. The one on the rear was looking straight at me and hollering something to the driver. No alarms tripped until I saw him suddenly bank left and accelerate into the turn. The computer in my head that does idle geometry and lead computations as I observe moving objects ran a quick calculation on the bike's curve. It wasn't heading for the middle of the opposite lane. It was heading for a close encounter with moi. A cowboy and his snatch, at last! My time, rate, and distance computer was now running millisecond updates. I had three seconds till impact.

One Mississippi…

The snatch's eyes are locked on me, watching intently for dangers and opportunities. I know if I make any move of preparation or defense he will abort his run. I keep my face forward, watching from behind dark lenses. Joe's cyclo lurches into movement. I have to know what the snatch is going to go for. I have to know ahead of time in order to make my move quickly enough.

Two Mississippi…

I've got a shopping bag at my feet, some miscellaneous stuff hanging out of my shirt pocket, a leather folder on my lap. Wearing no jewelry. So he's got three options. But I can't tell where his focus is. Damn! This is going to be close. Look to his grab hand. It's open and ready, waist-level and rising. So it won't be the shopping bag. I'm holding stone still. He's closing fast and on schedule. There! I can see his eyes. I can see the whites of them.

Three…

He seems to be looking me in the eyes. Is he going for my

shades? They'll steal anything, if only just for practice. I can hear the cowboy's engine, he's still winding up, accelerating. They'll make the grab and be gone in a heartbeat.

Miss…

There! I see it: the vector of the snatch's hand and eye. He's going for my hat! The bastard! My $80 handwoven-in-Ecuador, genuine Panama hat! That changes the whole game. It's one thing to nick a man's briefcase, but his hat is just too damned personal. He who steals my purse steals trash; but he who messes with my hat gets punished.

issi…

So now I want to hurt him. But how? I could stiff-arm the driver and spill them both onto the pavement. But they're coming too fast, I could dislocate my shoulder. His hand is up for the grab and I've got to decide. I could spit in his eye. But I might miss. Never been a good spitter. I could have tossed the shopping bag at their heads, but there's no time now. Head butt them? Scratch at their eyes? Call 'em names?

POW!

I high-fived the snatch as hard as I could. I know it was solid because it stung my own hand like frenzy. The force and surprise rotated the snatch's body counterclockwise around the axis of his spine more than ninety degrees. The motion translated the speeding vehicle's forward momentum into one wild and crazy ride. The driver almost lost it to the right, overcompensated to the left and straight into oncoming traffic. He slalomed back and forth across both lanes for one hundred yards, the snatch screaming and cursing like a jilted Latina.

Both Joe and I laughed our heads off. "How do you like that, you SOBs?" I hollered after them, waving my hat. "I win, you bastards! I win!"

"You win, Kieu! You win!" Joe shouted and laughed.

Joe didn't know precisely what game I had been playing, but it was abundantly clear to him that I had won. Hands down.

Richard Sterling is a writer, editor, lecturer, and insatiable traveler. Earlier in life he served in the Navy and was a Silicon Valley engineer, but stability and respectability lost out over wanderlust. Since taking up the pen he has been honored by the James Beard Foundation for his food writing, and by the Lowell Thomas Awards for his travel literature. He is the editor of Food: A Taste of the Road *and* The Adventure of Food, *and the author of several books in the Lonely Planet World Food series, as well as* The Fearless Diner *and* The Fire Never Dies, *from which this story was excerpted. He is based in Berkeley, California, where he is often politically incorrect.*

Acknowledgments

We would like to thank our families and friends for their usual forbearance while we are putting a book together. Many thanks also to Tim and Sean O'Reilly, Susan Brady, Krista Holmstrom, Raj Khadka, Jennifer Leo, Michele Wetherbee, Patty Holden, Judy Johnson, and Cindy Williams for their support and contributions to the book.

TRAVELERS' TALES

THE SOUL OF TRAVEL

Footsteps Series

THE FIRE NEVER DIES
One Man's Raucous Romp Down the Road of Food, Passion, and Adventure
By Richard Sterling
ISBN 1-885-211-70-8
$14.95

"Sterling's writing is like spitfire, foursquare and jazzy with crackle...."
—*Kirkus Reviews*

LAST TROUT IN VENICE
The Far-Flung Escapades of an Accidental Adventurer
By Doug Lansky
ISBN 1-885-211-63-5
$14.95

"Traveling with Doug Lansky might result in a considerably shortened life expectancy...but what a way to go." —Tony Wheeler, Lonely Planet Publications

ONE YEAR OFF
Leaving It All Behind for a Round-the-World Journey with Our Children
By David Elliot Cohen
ISBN 1-885-211-65-1
$14.95
A once-in-a-lifetime adventure generously shared.

THE WAY OF THE WANDERER
Discover Your True Self Through Travel
By David Yeadon
ISBN 1-885-211-60-0
$14.95

Experience transformation through travel with this delightful, illustrated collection by award-winning author David Yeadon.

TAKE ME WITH YOU
A Round-the-World Journey to Invite a Stranger Home
By Brad Newsham
ISBN 1-885-211-51-1
$24.00 (cloth)

"Newsham is an ideal guide. His journey, at heart, is into humanity." —Pico Iyer, author of *Video Night in Kathmandu*

KITE STRINGS OF THE SOUTHERN CROSS
A Woman's Travel Odyssey
By Laurie Gough
ISBN 1-885-211-54-6
$14.95 ——★ ★ ★——

ForeWord Silver Medal Winner
—*Travel Book of the Year*

THE SWORD OF HEAVEN
A Five Continent Odyssey to Save the World
By Mikkel Aaland
ISBN 1-885-211-44-9
$24.00 (cloth)
"Few books capture the soul of the road like *The Sword of Heaven*, a sharp-edged, beautifully rendered memoir that will inspire anyone." —Phil Cousineau, author of *The Art of Pilgrimage*

STORM
A Motorcycle Journey of Love, Endurance, and Transformation
By Allen Noren
ISBN 1-885-211-45-7
$24.00 (cloth) ——★ ★ ★——

ForeWord Gold Medal Winner
—*Travel Book of the Year*

Travelers' Tales Classics

COAST TO COAST
A Journey Across 1950s America
By Jan Morris
ISBN 1-885-211-79-1
$16.95

After reporting on the first Everest ascent in 1953, Morris spent a year journeying by car, train, ship, and aircraft across the United States. In her brilliant prose, Morris records with exuberance and curiosity a time of innocence in the U.S.

TRADER HORN
A Young Man's Astounding Adventures in 19th Century Equatorial Africa
By Alfred Aloysius Horn
ISBN 1-885-211-81-3
$16.95

Here is the stuff of legends —tale of thrills and danger, wild beasts, serpents, and savages. An unforgettable and vivid portrait of a vanished late-19th century Africa.

THE ROYAL ROAD TO ROMANCE
By Richard Halliburton
ISBN 1-885-211-53-8
$14.95

"Laughing at hardships, dreaming of beauty, ardent for adventure, Halliburton has managed to sing into the pages of this glorious book his own exultant spirit of youth and freedom."
— *Chicago Post*

UNBEATEN TRACKS IN JAPAN
By Isabella L. Bird
ISBN 1-885-211-57-0
$14.95

Isabella Bird was one of the most adventurous women travelers of the 19th century with journeys to Tibet, Canada, Korea, Turkey, Hawaii, and Japan. A fascinating read for anyone interested in women's travel, spirituality, and Asian culture.

THE RIVERS RAN EAST
By Leonard Clark
ISBN 1-885-211-66-X
$16.95

Clark is the original Indiana Jones, relaying a breathtaking account of his search for the legendary El Dorado gold in the Amazon.

Travel Humor

NOT SO FUNNY WHEN IT HAPPENED
The Best of Travel Humor and Misadventure
Edited by Tim Cahill
ISBN 1-885-211-55-4
$12.95

Laugh with Bill Bryson, Dave Barry, Anne Lamott, Adair Lara, and many more.

THERE'S NO TOILET PAPER...ON THE ROAD LESS TRAVELED
The Best of Travel Humor and Misadventure
Edited by Doug Lansky
ISBN 1-885-211-27-9
$12.95

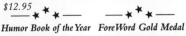

—★ ★—
Humor Book of the Year
—Independent Publisher's Book Award

—★ ★—
ForeWord Gold Medal Winner— Humor Book of the Year

LAST TROUT IN VENICE
The Far-Flung Escapades of an Accidental Adventurer
By Doug Lansky
ISBN 1-885-211-63-5
$14.95

"Traveling with Doug Lansky might result in a considerably shortened life expectancy...but what a way to go."
—Tony Wheeler, Lonely Planet Publications

Women's Travel

A WOMAN'S PASSION FOR TRAVEL
More True Stories from A Woman's World
Edited by Marybeth Bond & Pamela Michael
ISBN 1-885-211-36-8
$17.95

"A diverse and gripping series of stories!" —Arlene Blum, author of *Annapurna: A Woman's Place*

A WOMAN'S WORLD
True Stories of Life on the Road
Edited by Marybeth Bond
Introduction by Dervla Murphy
ISBN 1-885-211-06-6
$17.95

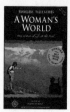

Winner of the Lowell Thomas Award for Best Travel Book— Society of American Travel Writers

WOMEN IN THE WILD
True Stories of Adventure and Connection
Edited by Lucy McCauley
ISBN 1-885-211-21-X
$17.95

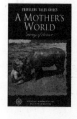

"A spiritual, moving, and totally female book to take you around the world and back." —*Mademoiselle*

A MOTHER'S WORLD
Journeys of the Heart
Edited by Marybeth Bond & Pamela Michael
ISBN 1-885-211-26-0
$14.95

"These stories remind us that motherhood is one of the great unifying forces in the world" —*San Francisco Examiner*

Food

ADVENTURES IN WINE
True Stories of Vineyards and Vintages around the World
Edited by Thom Elkjer
ISBN 1-885-211-80-5
$17.95

Humanity, community, and brotherhood comprise the marvelous virtues of the wine world. This collection toasts the warmth and wonders of this large, extended family in stories by travelers who are wine novices and experts alike.

FOOD (Updated)
A Taste of the Road
Edited by Richard Sterling
Introduction by Margo True
ISBN 1-885-211-77-5
$18.95

Silver Medal Winner of the Lowell Thomas Award for Best Travel Book—Society of American Travel Writers

HER FORK IN THE ROAD
Women Celebrate Food and Travel
Edited by Lisa Bach
ISBN 1-885-211-71-6
$16.95
A savory sampling of stories by some of the best writers in and out of the food and travel fields.

THE ADVENTURE OF FOOD
True Stories of Eating Everything
Edited by Richard Sterling
ISBN 1-885-211-37-6
$17.95

"These stories are bound to whet appetites for more than food."

—*Publishers Weekly*

Spiritual Travel

THE SPIRITUAL GIFTS OF TRAVEL
The Best of Travelers' Tales
Edited by James O'Reilly and Sean O'Reilly
ISBN 1-885-211-69-4
$16.95

A collection of favorite stories of transformation on the road from our award-winning Travelers' Tales series that shows the myriad ways travel indelibly alters our inner landscapes.

THE WAY OF THE WANDERER
Discover Your True Self Through Travel
By David Yeadon
ISBN 1-885-211-60-0
$14.95

Experience transformation through travel with this delightful, illustrated collection by award-winning author David Yeadon.

PILGRIMAGE
Adventures of the Spirit
Edited by Sean O'Reilly & James O'Reilly
Introduction by Phil Cousineau
ISBN 1-885-211-56-2
$16.95

———— ✱✱✱ ————

ForeWord Silver Medal Winner
— Travel Book of the Year

A WOMAN'S PATH
Women's Best Spiritual Travel Writing
Edited by Lucy McCauley, Amy G. Carlson & Jennifer Leo
ISBN 1-885-211-48-1
$16.95

"A sensitive exploration of women's lives that have been unexpectedly and spiritually touched by travel experiences…. Highly recommended."
—Library Journal

THE ROAD WITHIN
True Stories of Transformation and the Soul
Edited by Sean O'Reilly, James O'Reilly & Tim O'Reilly
ISBN 1-885-211-19-8
$17.95

———— ✱✱✱ ————

Best Spiritual Book — Independent Publisher's Book Award

THE ULTIMATE JOURNEY
Inspiring Stories of Living and Dying
James O'Reilly, Sean O'Reilly & Richard Sterling
ISBN 1-885-211-38-4
$17.95

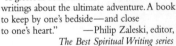

"A glorious collection of writings about the ultimate adventure. A book to keep by one's bedside—and close to one's heart."   —Philip Zaleski, editor, *The Best Spiritual Writing series*

Adventure

TESTOSTERONE PLANET
True Stories from a Man's World
Edited by Sean O'Reilly, Larry Habegger & James O'Reilly
ISBN 1-885-211-43-0
$17.95

Thrills and laughter with some of today's best writers: Sebastian Junger, Tim Cahill, Bill Bryson, and Jon Krakauer.

DANGER!
True Stories of Trouble and Survival
Edited by James O'Reilly, Larry Habegger & Sean O'Reilly
ISBN 1-885-211-32-5
$17.95

"Exciting…for those who enjoy living on the edge or prefer to read the survival stories of others, this is a good pick."
—Library Journal

Special Interest

365 TRAVEL
A Daily Book of Journeys, Meditations, and Adventures
Edited by Lisa Bach
ISBN 1-885-211-67-8
$14.95

An illuminating collection of travel wisdom and adventures that reminds us all of the lessons we learn while on the road.

THE GIFT OF RIVERS
True Stories of Life on the Water
Edited by Pamela Michael
Introduction by Robert Hass
ISBN 1-885-211-42-2
$14.95

"*The Gift of Rivers* is a soulful compendium of wonderful stories that illuminate, educate, inspire, and delight."
—David Brower, Chairman of Earth Island Institute

FAMILY TRAVEL
The Farther You Go, the Closer You Get
Edited by Laura Manske
ISBN 1-885-211-33-3
$17.95

"This is family travel at its finest." —*Working Mother*

LOVE & ROMANCE
True Stories of Passion on the Road
Edited by Judith Babcock Wylie
ISBN 1-885-211-18-X
$17.95

"A wonderful book to read by a crackling fire."
—*Romantic Traveling*

THE GIFT OF BIRDS
True Encounters with Avian Spirits
Edited by Larry Habegger & Amy G. Carlson
ISBN 1-885-211-41-4
$17.95

"These are all wonderful, entertaining stories offering a *bird's-eye view!* of our avian friends."
—*Booklist*

A DOG'S WORLD
True Stories of Man's Best Friend on the Road
Edited by Christine Hunsicker
ISBN 1-885-211-23-6
$12.95

This extraordinary collection includes stories by John Steinbeck, Helen Thayer, James Herriot, Pico Iyer, and many others.

THE GIFT OF TRAVEL
The Best of Travelers' Tales
Edited by Larry Habegger, James O'Reilly & Sean O'Reilly
ISBN 1-885-211-25-2
$14.95

"Like gourmet chefs in a French market, the editors of Travelers' Tales pick, sift, and prod their way through the weighty shelves of contemporary travel writing, creaming off the very best."

—William Dalrymple, author of *City of Djinns*

Travel Advice

SHITTING PRETTY
How to Stay Clean and Healthy While Traveling
By Dr. Jane Wilson-Howarth
ISBN 1-885-211-47-3
$12.95

A light-hearted book about a serious subject for millions of travelers— staying healthy on the road—written by international health expert, Dr. Jane Wilson-Howarth.

THE FEARLESS SHOPPER
How to Get the Best Deals on the Planet
By Kathy Borrus
ISBN 1-885-211-39-2
$14.95

"Anyone who reads *The Fearless Shopper* will come away a smarter, more responsible shopper and a more curious, culturally attuned traveler."
—Jo Mancuso, *The Shopologist*

GUTSY WOMEN
More Travel Tips and Wisdom for the Road
By Marybeth Bond
ISBN 1-885-211-61-9
$12.95

Second Edition—Packed with funny, instructive, and inspiring advice for women heading out to see the world.

SAFETY AND SECURITY FOR WOMEN WHO TRAVEL
By Sheila Swan & Peter Laufer
ISBN 1-885-211-29-5
$12.95

A must for every woman traveler!

THE FEARLESS DINER
Travel Tips and Wisdom for Eating around the World
By Richard Sterling
ISBN 1-885-211-22-8
$7.95

Combines practical advice on foodstuffs, habits, and etiquette, with hilarious accounts of others' eating adventures.

THE PENNY PINCHER'S PASSPORT TO LUXURY TRAVEL
The Art of Cultivating Preferred Customer Status
By Joel L. Widzer
ISBN 1-885-211-31-7
$12.95

Proven techniques on how to travel first class at discount prices, even if you're not a frequent flyer.

GUTSY MAMAS
Travel Tips and Wisdom for Mothers on the Road
By Marybeth Bond
ISBN 1-885-211-20-1
$7.95

A delightful guide for mothers traveling with their children— or without them!

Destination Titles:
True Stories of Life on the Road

AMERICA
Edited by Fred Setterberg
ISBN 1-885-211-28-7
$19.95

FRANCE (Updated)
Edited by James O'Reilly,
Larry Habegger &
Sean O'Reilly
ISBN 1-885-211-73-2
$18.95

AMERICAN
SOUTHWEST
Edited by Sean O'Reilly
& James O'Reilly
ISBN 1-885-211-58-9
$17.95

GRAND CANYON
Edited by Sean O'Reilly,
James O'Reilly &
Larry Habegger
ISBN 1-885-211-34-1
$17.95

AUSTRALIA
Edited by Larry Habegger
ISBN 1-885-211-40-6
$17.95

GREECE
Edited by Larry Habegger,
Sean O'Reilly &
Brian Alexander
ISBN 1-885-211-52-X
$17.95

BRAZIL
Edited by Annette Haddad
& Scott Doggett
Introduction by Alex
Shoumatoff
ISBN 1-885-211-11-2
$17.95

HAWAI'I
Edited by Rick &
Marcie Carroll
ISBN 1-885-211-35-X
$17.95

CENTRAL AMERICA
Edited by Larry Habegger
& Natanya Pearlman
ISBN 1-885-211-74-0
$17.95

HONG KONG
Edited by James O'Reilly,
Larry Habegger &
Sean O'Reilly
ISBN 1-885-211-03-1
$17.95

CUBA
Edited by Tom Miller
ISBN 1-885-211-62-7
$17.95

INDIA
Edited by James O'Reilly
& Larry Habegger
ISBN 1-885-211-01-5
$17.95

IRELAND
Edited by James O'Reilly,
Larry Habegger &
Sean O'Reilly
ISBN 1-885-211-46-5
$17.95

SAN FRANCISCO
Edited by James O'Reilly,
Larry Habegger &
Sean O'Reilly
ISBN 1-885-211-08-2
$17.95

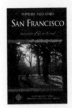

ITALY (Updated)
Edited by Anne Calcagno
Introduction by Jan Morris
ISBN 1-885-211-72-4
$18.95

SPAIN (Updated)
Edited by Lucy McCauley
ISBN 1-885-211-78-3
$19.95

JAPAN
Edited by Donald W. George
& Amy G. Carlson
ISBN 1-885-211-04-X
$17.95

THAILAND (Updated)
Edited by James O'Reilly
& Larry Habegger
ISBN 1-885-211-75-9
$18.95

MEXICO (Updated)
Edited by James O'Reilly
& Larry Habegger
ISBN 1-885-211-59-7
$17.95

TIBET
Edited by James O'Reilly,
Larry Habegger, & Kim
Morris
ISBN 1-885-211-76-7
$18.95

NEPAL
Edited by Rajendra
S. Khadka
ISBN 1-885-211-14-7
$17.95

TUSCANY
Edited by James O'Reilly, &
Tara Austen Weaver
ISBN 1-885-211-68-6
$16.95

PARIS
Edited by James O'Reilly,
Larry Habegger &
Sean O'Reilly
ISBN 1-885-211-10-4
$17.95